# GOLF ON THE HILL

## John Reece

**White Tree
Books**

First published in 1991 by
WHITE TREE BOOKS
an imprint of REDCLIFFE PRESS LTD.,
49 Park Street, Bristol BS1 5NT

ISBN 1 872971 02 4

Typeset and printed by The Longdunn Press Ltd., Bristol.

# Contents

# Acknowledgements

The author wishes to thank a number of people for their help in putting together this history of golf on Coombe Hill.

It was Mrs Anne Hewer, of Vine House, Henbury, daughter of Hiatt and Abigail Baker, who provided verification of family details and contributed the wedding photograph of her parents. Miss Agnes Skyrme and Mrs Irene Wiltshire, both of Westbury, added much to the colouring of the village scene with pictures and stories. Miss Skyrme's brother, Arthur, was one of the real characters of the club, and Mrs Wiltshire's father, Ernest Mogford, was a kingpin of village life and the artisan section.

Mrs Alma Robertson, of the Ladies Golf Union, St Andrews, was extremely and cheerfully helpful in providing a wealth of detail and a collection of fine photographs concerning Phyllis Lobbett, of whom the club knew nothing; and Mrs Ruth Mary Stewart of Padstow contributed invaluable pictures of her late father, C.H. Young.

It is a pleasure to acknowledge the debt owed to Mrs P.M. Denney, of the Society of Merchant Venturers of Bristol, for her collection of "sundry Bakers", and thanks go to Miss Wanda Morgan, one of the country's great golfers of the past, who now lives at Whitstable and reminisces so entertainingly.

W. (Bill) Rangecroft, and George Prescott, have contributed mightily to the book, and thanks are due to the Rev. Ronald Cowley and Peter Powesland, for research on our behalf; similarly to R.A.L. (Bobby) Burnet, historian and librarian to the Royal and Ancient Club of St Andrews; and the Bristol Reference Library.

Without the artistic talents and inspired support of Vic Parkes and his wife, Barbara, the author would not have experienced the happiness he feels at the end product. And finally to his wife, Peggy, who pointed a way when it seemed that there wasn't one.

# Message from the Chairman

The last quarter of the 19th century saw a great expansion of the game in Britain with the number of clubs rising from less than 100 in 1875 to 1300 in 1900. Amongst them was Henbury, which shares with Bristol & Clifton the distinction of being the oldest club in the Bristol area still in existence, with Bath (1880) leading the way in the West Country.

Your Committee felt we should have a permanent record in book form of the history of the Club, its origins, traumas and growth, and we were fortunate to have among our members a first class journalist in John Reece who readily agreed to undertake what proved a mammoth task because of the lack of any comprehensive records.

With his journalistic skills he combines a love of the game and a devotion to Henbury, which he joined after war service in 1946. He has been a single figure player for over 50 years and many sound judges feel that but for war service he would have been capped for England. Now in his middle 70s his ambition for 1991 is to get back to single figures. Freed from the labours of this time-consuming project—why not?

By dint of much research in the Bristol Central Library, interviews with anybody who might have relationships with former and original Henbury members, chasing reluctant solicitors to look up ancient deeds and even contacting that august body, the Ladies Golf Union at St Andrews (they were most helpful) he has amassed the various details.

In some respects not a lot has changed – the boxes down below still find their way into the Trym, the public still walk the course oblivious to the dangers, and for obvious reasons like our teams of yesteryear the party to the county dinner travelled by mini-bus. All of us, especially those who have come from other parts of the country (immigrants or missionaries, according to your way of thinking), must thank their original pioneers for leaving us such an inspiring legacy.

I am sure you will enjoy the book and the tales of characters old and new (we still have some around). It is a first-rate introduction to what I hope will be an excellent year. The details of the various events will be fully publicised and I hope everyone will take part in at least some of them and show the spirit of friendliness for which the club has always been renowned to all our various visitors.

Chairman R.G. (Bob) Harvie.

# Prologue

The topmost leaves of the oak and ash standing high at the back of the fourth green danced and rippled in the bright sunlight.

To the illustrious player standing upon the tee there was beyond doubt a breeze to consider. He could not feel it but he could see its effects, and he made his stroke accordingly. He was utterly confounded when the ball went into a bunker. There was no wind.

As he passed beneath them, having recovered his par figure with the utmost competence, the leaves still fluttered and waved, almost it seemed in derisive glee. He stared upwards in disbelief before going on his way, intent on other matters but unable to resist a further backward glance and another shake of the head.

Unseen presences mingled with the spectators that day, flitting from group to group, marvelling at the transformation since their own mortal shapes had brought the game of golf to this place. A hundred years had passed "like an evening gone".

Later, as shadows lengthened over the course and people dispersed, lights came on in the clubhouse where a young man and his friends celebrated a victory.

When the sun slipped down behind the tops of the trees leaves rustled softly as the presences glided away.

They had been here, "absent in body, but present in spirit," the Arthurians who bequeathed to us this precious heritage.

*Arthur Waters*
*Feby 26th 1894*          *Arthur Robinson.*

# Up the Hill

The villagers of Henbury and Westbury were accustomed to the sight of people carrying golf clubs on the way up the Hill for a long time before a club was formed. This is borne out by the fact that as soon as it happened on December 10th, 1891, handicaps were disclosed proving fore-knowledge of the game. The men and women concerned had obviously played before, if only on Coombe Hill, and within weeks competitions were in full swing and matches were played with other clubs in the district.

Whole families became involved in the game's development here. At the time of the first meeting there were 21 members, and of these nine couples were married.

Coombe Hill, the plateau of fields high between the villages, belonged to John Harford, owner of Blaise Castle. Cattle and sheep roamed there from the farm where Hyland Grove stands. Because there was no shelter except under the trees, Harford gave his golfing friends access to Blaise Lodge.

Nothing in the sparse records indicates any clamour or pressure for the formation of a club, and it was not until the evening of Thursday, December 10th, 1891, that Charles Way, the vicar's son, wrote in a new minute book procured for the occasion – and still with us – that "The First General Meeting . . . was held at the Vicarage, Mr Arthur Robinson in the chair".

What followed gave further indication that golf had been going on for some time because –

The Meeting proceeded to discuss certain rules proposed by C.P. Way. Numerous Rules and Regulations having been agreed upon it was arranged that these should be printed in a convenient form and a copy sent to every member as soon as possible.

The following officers and committee were elected for the year 1892: President, Arthur Baker Esq; Vice-President, Arthur Robinson Esq; Treasurer, Mrs Way; Secretary, C.P. Way. Committee: H. Baker Esq, Herbert Edwards Esq, Walter Jefferis Esq, Mrs Robinson, Mrs Henry Matthews, Mrs Fedden.

There is no doubt Baker was the driving force in this little community. He was 50 years old, and lived with his wife, Amy Mary, and their son Edgar in Henbury Hill House. He was one of the leading corn merchants and millers of his day, and it was his custom to ride on horseback from home to his mills in Redcliff Backs. He was probably glad to get this golf launch behind him because in 1892 he was to be High Sheriff of Bristol, and there would not be too much time . . .

It was natural enough for the Vicarage to be used for the first meeting because it was home to Mrs Way and her son, Charles, and they were doing the paper work after all. She was the wife of John Hugh Way who was ordained deacon in 1859 and succeeded his father, Henry Hugh, as vicar of Henbury the following year.

Charles was 21, and it was his ambition to follow his father. In a short while he would leave the village to be assistant curate in other parishes before becoming vicar of Henbury himself, which happened in 1906.

That he had some knowledge of golf is obvious from his assertive remarks at the first annual meeting, and it was equally plain that his mother had some experience of it.

Charles was shortly to marry Ethel Mary Danks from Wolverhampton, and they went away for some years until 1906 when he became vicar. His parents continued to live in the Vicarage, and Charles, his wife and son moved in at "the parsonage in the village," a house called The White Lodge, now also known as 266 Henbury Road. When his father died in 1912 Charles and his family moved into the Vicarage themselves. The following year a daughter, Abigail Mary, was born.

The appointment of Mrs Way as the first treasurer confirmed the equal footing on which men and women entered the golfing adventure. It has been a long standing belief in some quarters that the Henbury Ladies Club came first, but it is not so. Five years were to pass before the ladies had what they could call their own course.

---

*Footnote*: Everything for golf at Geo Plum and Co's Dolphin Street, Bristol. Illustrated prize lists, post free.

# Just imagine . . .

It takes little imagination to picture the scene in the following months when members gathered for a game.

To get there was a simple walk for most of the original members who lived almost in sight of the fields, but soon there were others from further afield, from Durdham Park, Clifton, Redland and Horfield Barracks. And Maud Matthews came in from as far as Newport Tower, Berkeley. Did Miss Matthews make this journey alone by horse and trap, one wonders? Where had she learned about golf? Was she related to Mr and Mrs Henry Matthews? There are no answers, but speculation is entertaining.

Bear in mind there was no Falcondale Road, no residential Canford Lane but a long, narrow country road with tall hedges. The journey from Horfield was across open country, and the walk over the Downs culminated in the threading of a path through fields and lanes, past farms and barns in the lovely Westbury valley to reach Henbury Hill. People walked or rode to Coombe Hill, carrying their clubs, like pilgrims making their way to some holy place.

There were two tracks on Coombe Hill, one leading from Henbury Road past the site of the present clubhouse until it turned left at the hedge at the back of our eleventh green. It followed the hedge across the 18th fairway and down through the woods. The other came out of the woods on the right of the 15th fairway and went in an almost straight line to the 17th tee where it also disappeared into the woods.

The place where golfers gathered was in the centre of the plateau, roughly where our eleventh tee stands. One or two elms there afforded some shelter and provided a focal point. A little more imagination can conjure the sight of horses tethered beneath the trees, or in nearby woods, propped up bicycles, baskets, bags, shoes, boots and all sorts of paraphernalia scattered around as players paired off for a game. First tee scenes. Men and women swinging clubs in all directions, laughing and excited at the start of a great adventure.

Coombe Hill is wide open today. A hundred years ago the fields were closed in by walls or hedges. Trees and dense undergrowth filled every aspect except for the wonderful view across Westbury to the Downs. All this fore-shortened distance, and the hedge across the course from the back of our eleventh gave an impression of boundary.

In winter it must have been a dripping, misty, overgrown area, rather forbidding and desolate. In summer it was a favourite place for family walks and picnics, a fine playground for children, with sheep and cattle grazing. In one or two places there was quarrying, notably at the Henbury Road end on the course side of The Lodge, and in the hillside in front of our present tenth tee, but golf did not extend down there until much later.

Elsewhere in 1891 golf was not played extensively and there were not really many good courses, but the sport quickly acquired the reputation as a rich man's game that was to tarnish it for years.

It is true that landed gentry dominated it in many places, men who dressed accordingly in tall silk hats, swallow-tail coats of many colours, and tight trousers. The Henbury stock looked quite different, as may be gathered from pictures of sporting caps, knickerbockers, jackets, collars and ties and substantial, cleated boots. The ladies wore skirts to the ground, blouses with nipped-in waists, boaters, and flat shoes.

If there was a feeling throughout the country that men did not approve of women playing golf it was far from the case here.

---

*Footnote*: Ladies' tournament, Tuesday, October 25th, 1892, won by Miss Emmeline Cave, nett 127, handicap 9; Saturday, November 12th, match with Thornbury won by nine holes – A. Robinson, Major Langford, B. Matthews, C.P. Way, W. Jefferis, A. Gwynne. Saturday December 10th (anniversary) match with Thornbury won by six holes.

# Lodgings

Sheep kept the grass down, but teeing areas and greens had to be cut, and it is likely that the farmer or someone from the estate gave a hand in this.

Tees were simply convenient patches of level ground chosen on the basis of "let's drive from here!" The grass was cut or trampled by the clodhopping boots, and the greens were larger areas, not so level but cut shorter. The only way to tell one from the other was by size and the fact that one had a flagstick stuck in a hole. Cutting holes was a problem, too, and we do not know how it was done.

Nothing remained so crude for very long because as soon as the club was formed competitive golf with others became routine. Thornbury was operating before Henbury, and the Downs club was going strong.

Medal competitions were called handicaps, as good a name as any come to think of it, and matches were decided by the number of holes up. For instance, a match would always go to 18 holes and the number of holes up at the end would be the score. This sometimes gave shattering results like: Henbury Gentlemen 21, Thornbury Gentlemen 0.

Arthur Robinson played Winfield Robinson of Thornbury (apparently no relation) in one of the first games and won 7-0. But he would have won 4 and 3 by our standards. He got to seven by winning the last three holes.

Full use was made of The Lodge, but the situation could not persist in spite of Harford's generosity. The shambles on wet and windy days can be imagined, and as winter approached the members pressed for some form of accommodation as a club.

On October 6th it was decided unanimously to do something, and by the time of the annual meeting on January 14th, 1893, an iron hut was put up, the money being subscribed by members. Although there is no description available, the rather grand title of The Golf House was bestowed upon it.

This acquisition led to the changing of Rule 7, the words "Blaise Castle Lodge" being deleted and "Golf Hut" inserted in their place. House or hut, it was decided that "for the protection of members' and club property, keys left in the door of the Golf House shall be handed over to the Ground Man from whom the owners may obtain them on payment of one shilling."

Charles Way was pleased to remark in his first report as secretary that "instead of being in debt, as is the way of most young clubs, we have a balance in hand of £3.7s.10¾d." He made it sound as if other clubs were not in such a healthy condition.

Several early improvements were made, with lockers installed in the hut and the provision of white discs at the teeing grounds, but it was deplored that the dry summer was bad for levelling greens or tees. The Ground Man, as Way described him, was named Comer, in whose hands rested the early course maintenance.

A glance at Mrs Way's financial report shows that £17.10.6. was paid to Comer, and that various items were provided for the greater advancement of the club. Two of these arouse curiosity – the relatively enormous payment of £5 to a Mr Cooper, and £1.0.6. to a Mrs Lodge. Cooper was almost certainly the farmer whose cattle roamed the range, but Mrs L. remains the sort of mystery only a Miss Marple could solve.

Way was hard-hitting in criticism of the standard of play in the first year which suggests once more that he was familiar with the game elsewhere. "As regards the play of members," he said at the annual meeting, "there is no doubt that it does not improve as it should. A score of 46 is the men's record when it should be nearer 36. The ladies have much more to be proud of," he went on, "with their record at 49, only three worse than the men. Putting is the weak point of members generally, and should be improved in 1893."

When the election of officers and committee for 1893 took place Baker and Robinson remained president and vice-president, but Mrs Way stood down as treasurer and Charles took over. The new secretary was Bertram Henry Matthews, a printer from Shirehampton who, with his wife, was a founder member.

In the years ahead Matthews was to play a prominent part in Bristol golf, and forty years after starting at Henbury he became president of Shirehampton Park.

The committee was Hiatt Baker, Jefferis, Ormston Pease, who was on the point of buying Henbury Court, Mrs

*Left*, Hiatt Baker and his bride, Abigail Dorothea, sister of Charles Way, photographed in the Vicarage garden after the ceremony. *Above*, Hiatt Cowles Baker.

Robinson, Mrs Matthews and Mrs Fedden. A number of officers from Horfield Barracks joined the club, notably Major Langford and his wife, who were later to play leading roles, a Captain Taylor and a Mr W.H. de B. Griffith, probaby a subaltern. By the time Langford won the November handicap with a gross 103 he was a colonel.

It is fascinating to study the list of 56 members written up in the first log book, which ends in 1897 and is the only men's record to survive the 1959 fire that destroyed the rest of the records.

Many bore names of distinction or were destined to become such in west country life. Henry Vincent Fedden, who was a magistrate, and his wife, the new committee member, had a son, Romilley, who was not apparently a golfer but became famous as a painter and later produced several books on art and fishing. Charles Henry Cave, of Rodway Hill House, Mangotsfield, was a son of Sir Charles Daniel Cave, J.P., a banker who was High Sheriff of Bristol in 1859 and lived in Clifton Park. John Harford was a banker descended from John Scandrett Harford, of Brunswick Square. The Henbury Harford and his wife and daughter were original club members. William Charles Beloe of the Clifton family was a merchant, and the list goes on . . .

There were sundry Bakers, not all related. Indeed it is difficult to trace one or two, but the principals as far as we are concerned were Arthur and Hiatt. Arthur had an only son, Edgar Arthur, later to become secretary, and an eminent elder brother, William Proctor, a partner in the family business and Mayor of Bristol in 1871–2.

Hiatt Cowles Baker, who lived at Hallen Lodge, was not related to Arthur, but was son of the late W. Mills Baker, J.P. of The Holmes, Stoke Bishop, and cousin of Herbert Midelton Baker, who later lived at the same address and joined the club in 1894.

In 1884 Hiatt became head of Baker Baker & Co, the linen drapers, when he was only 21. Three years later he played rugby for England. He was an enthusiastic climber and member of the Alpine Club, and he was passionately fond of gardening. He was 28 when the club was formed, and in 1895 married Abigail Dorothea, the sister of Charles Way. They lived at Oaklands, Almondsbury. Their daughter is Mrs Anne Hewer who now lives at Vine House, Henbury, and who confirms her mother's early interest in golf. A year before her marriage Abigail was a committee member.

A common bond among the Henbury men apart from golf seemed to be membership of the Society of Merchant Venturers.

16

# Nine Holes

*The Golfing Annual* of 1893–4 listed Henbury for the first time:

Entrance fee, £1.1.0. for Family, and Ten Shillings and Sixpence for Single Subscribers. Annual Subscription, £2.2s. for Family, and £1.1s. for Single Subscribers. Number of Members, 19 Family and 23 Single Members. The membership is restricted to residents in Henbury and 40 members outside.

The record is 86 for two rounds, by W. Jefferis, in November, 1893.

The course, which consists of nine holes, is situated on Coombe Hill, near Bristol, about two and a half miles from Clifton Down Station. Fees for visitors (introduced by members) 1s. One day, 2s.6d. a month.

Club activity was routine by all accounts in 1893, with matches home and away with Thornbury, Filton, Clifton II and Clifton Ladies. Conditions were laid down for handicaps (medals) that the entrance fee should be 1s., that no prize should exceed 10s., and further – "That after every handicap the Handicap committee shall carefully consider the points of players."

In other words, it was necessary even then to look out for bandits!

It was decided to keep a suggestion book in the hut, and one wishes that had survived.

There was a rumpus that October when indignant members protested against some of their fellows and the committee came out with the following:

As some member or members have taken and forgotten to return golf balls, etc., members are respectfully

On January 20th a Handicap was played per Rule 18. There were 14 entries, & ever played - Fine but very windy. Following were the scores :-

| | 1st Round | 2nd Round | Gross | H'cap |
|---|---|---|---|---|
| Miss E. Cave (Visitor) | 73 | 64 | 137 | 60 |
| " A. Way | 54 | 53 | 107 | 25 |
| Mr. H. Matthews | 76 | 78 | 154 | 70 |
| Mr. E. Baker | 60 | 60 | 120 | 36 |
| Miss K. Matthews | 78 | 72 | 150 | 65 |
| " G. Baker | 73 | 64 | 137 | 45 |
| " E. Baker | 67 | 71 | 138 | 45 |
| Mr. W. Jefferis | 57 | 49 | 106 | 13 |
| " A. M. Miller | 56 | 62 | 118 | 22 |
| " B. Matthews | 60 | 56 | 116 | 18 |
| " R. Deane | 59 | 57 | 116 | 16 |
| Miss E. Hill | | no | return | 26 |
| Capt Salvesen | | " | " | 16 |
| Mr. H. C. Baker | | | " | 33 |

*Above*, early handicaps. *Right*, two of Bill Branch's score cards.

GENTLEMEN.  Player Mr J Branch  H'cap  Strokes rec'd  Competition  Date June 29th

| Hole | Length | Bogey | Strokes Rec'd | Stroke Holes | Score | Won+Lost=Hlv'd 0 | Hole | Length | Bogey | Strokes Rec'd | Stroke Holes | Score | Won+Lost=Hlv'd 0 |
|---|---|---|---|---|---|---|---|---|---|---|---|---|---|
| 1 | 429 | 5 | 11 | | 4 | | 10 | 397 | 4 | 10 | | 4 | |
| 2 | 354 | 4 | 5 | | 4 | | 11 | 140 | 3 | 17 | | 2 | |
| 3 | 248 | 4 | 15 | | 4 | | 12 | 209 | 3 | 6 | | | |
| 4 | 345 | 4 | 9 | | 3 | | 13 | 486 | 5 | 2 | | 5 | |
| 5 | 141 | 3 | 18 | | 3 | | 14 | 449 | 5 | 8 | | 4 | |
| 6 | 474 | 5 | 7 | | 3 | | 15 | 169 | 3 | 12 | | 2 | |
| 7 | 442 | 5 | 3 | | 2 | | 16 | 284 | 4 | 14 | | 5 | |
| 8 | 311 | 4 | 13 | | 2 | | 17 | 330 | 4 | 4 | | 4 | |
| 9 | 182 | 3 | 1 | | 0 | | 18 | 267 | 4 | 16 | | 4 | |
| Totals Out | 2937 | 37 | | | 30 | | Totals Out | 2731 | 35 | | | 3 | |

*BOGEY SCORE   *E.G. A player receiving 9 strokes takes them at holes marked with figures 9 and under.

Holes +
Holes —

In bogey play the scores must be entered, otherwise the hole will be counted as lost.

STROKE SCORE
Home — 9?
Out — 30
Total — 90
Handicap — 60

Result   Certified by J Evans   Net —

‹———— THIS CARD MEASURES SIX INCHES ACROSS ————›

GENTLEMEN   **HENBURY GOLF CLUB**   Date 1928 (MAY)
Player W. J. BRANCH   H'cap   Strokes rec'd   Competition

| HOLE | Bogey | Length | Strokes Rec'd | Stroke Holes | Score | Won+Lost=Hlv'd | Putts | HOLE | Bogey | Length | Strokes Rec'd | Stroke Holes | Score | Won+Lost=Hlv'd |
|---|---|---|---|---|---|---|---|---|---|---|---|---|---|---|
| 1 HENBURY HILL | 5 | 429 | 11 | | 4 | | | 10 PUNCH BOWL | 4 | 397 | 10 | | 3 | |
| 2 CLUB HOUSE | 4 | 364 | 5 | | 5 | | | 11 DROP | 3 | 140 | 17 | | 3 | |
| 3 BEECHES | 4 | 248 | 15 | | 3 | | | 12 CHERRY ORCH'D | 3 | 209 | 6 | | 3 | |
| 4 QUARRY | 5 | 474 | 7 | | 4 | | | 13 LONG | 5 | 486 | 2 | | 5 | |
| 5 BLAIZE WOOD | 5 | 442 | 3 | | 4 | | | 14 RIDGE | 5 | 449 | 8 | | 4 | |
| 6 DOG'S LEG | 4 | 311 | 13 | | 3 | | | 15 TRYM | 3 | 169 | 12 | | 3 | |
| 7 COPPICE | 3 | 141 | 18 | | 3 | | | 16 VALLEY | 4 | 284 | 14 | | 4 | |
| 8 COOMBE DINGLE | 4 | 346 | 9 | | 3 | | | 17 ALLOTMENTS | 4 | 330 | 4 | | 4 | |
| 9 OAK TREE | 3 | 182 | 1 | | 3 | | | 18 HOME | 4 | 267 | 16 | | 3 | |
| TOTALS OUT | 37 | 2937 | | | 33 | | | TOTALS HOME | 35 | 7731 | | | | |

BOGEY SCORE   *E.G. A player receiving 9 strokes takes them at holes marked with figures 9 and under.

Holes +
Holes —

In bogey play the score must be entered, otherwise the hole will be counted as lost.

STROKE SCORE
Home 32
Out 33
Total 65
Handicap

Certified by E I M DAVEY

Result   Net —

‹———— THIS CARD MEASURES SIX INCHES ACROSS ————›

18

asked not to forget that the contents of the lockers are private property and must not be borrowed without the owner's permission.

There was still not enough room, and after great discussion at the start of 1894 the committee decided to have as many new lockers as possible made for the hut, with locks, and also to have a shelter built behind the hut for the caddies. This was the first mention of caddies, and there were to be twelve "who shall wear badges, and who shall be under the supervision of the professional".

This was fine, but there wasn't a professional. So it was decided to engage one in the place of Comer, the Ground Man who wasn't a professional at all. Still, we are not in a position to question this, or argue about it. The fact remains that Arthur Robinson, having some connection with the Burnham and Berrow club, no doubt by virtue of the Old Boy Network, was "to engage a young fellow from there at 15s. a week, to come at once to Henbury and be taken on until the end of May".

What is more, he was to be allowed to charge 1s. for playing a round of nine holes, "and a ball to be put down for him". He was also to be allowed to sell new balls – Silvertowns Best or A.I. – at 1s. each. A further bonus for the lucky chap would be the concession that he could do repaints at 3d. each of balls given him by members.

Seven days later, on January 20th, 1894, John Pople of Burnham was appointed grounds man and professional at 15s. a week, but it was also mutually arranged that he should charge 6d, not 1s. for nine holes. Comer got two weeks' notice, but whether or not that decision was mutual is not known.

Beyond the fact that Pople came from Burnham nothing was known of him. The Professional Golfers' Association at The Belfry has no record of him. And although Mr Mick Pople of Westbury-on-Trym, admits (1990) to "umpteen Poples in the family at Burnham, where we originated, your chap was not one of them".

Pople's qualifications were never disclosed, for perhaps the simple reason that the name of his Burnham master had little significance so far. In 1894 J.H. Taylor had yet to achieve his great fame, but he had been at Burnham since 1891 and clearly, if Pople could play golf, J.H. probably taught him. This explains how Henbury's new man came to play so well in the next 18 years.

# Red Caps

"Hold everything!" was the cry – or its equivalent – a month later when it was realised there was no room for more lockers in the hut, but it is not clear whether or not the order had been placed. Another decision was the provision of red caps instead of badges for the caddies.

Amid all these teething problems there arrived on the scene a Major Archdale, whose membership was proposed by Colonel Langford, and right away the good major was playing top for the club against Weston Seconds.

Saturday, March 3rd was "a magnificent day with only a slight breeze, but it resulted in a disastrous defeat for Henbury Gentlemen, owing, presumably, to a large extent to the fact that several of our team had never played on a sandy course before. Only seven a side played, as one of their men did not turn up.

"Our team went down by the 1.18 from Bristol and started playing directly on arrival, with the exception of B.H. Matthews who played at 12 o'clock."

The result was defeat by 45-0, remembering that scoring was the aggregate of holes won. The following week Henbury entertained Stinchcombe Hill second team and won by 17 holes.

To play a match at Weston involved arrangements that would be intolerable in any order of life today. The journey from Henbury meant getting to Clifton Down either by horse carriage, cycling or walking at least some part of the way. The likelihood is that the team met at some member's home and from there hired a cab or carriage for seven, with clubs and essential clothing. And then there was the business of getting home . . .

When the ladies went to Stinchcombe Hill to play six a side "Our team went up by the 10.20 from Clifton Down to Berkeley Road, and drove from there to the bottom of Stinchcombe Hill." It must be presumed they were met there, but the account does not tell us.

"Play commenced after lunch provided in the clubhouse. After tea we drove back to Berkeley Road in time to catch the 5.37. It was a dull afternoon with a sharp storm when the second round was being played."

The next ladies' match was at Bath. "Our team went up by the 1.0 from Bristol, and came back by the GWR after having some tea after the match – a dull afternoon with some storms."

On another occasion, "The ladies and gentlemen travelled in horse brakes (spelt 'breaks' in the recorded account), leaving Black Boy Hill at 12.30, Henbury Hill House at 1.0 and arriving at the Thornbury links about 2.30. Cost of break, including the driver, 30s."

When Weston ladies came up for a match on April 14th they arrived at Clifton Down at 12.05 and were driven over to the Vicarage where Mrs Way gave them lunch. "The afternoon became bright and warm after a soaking morning, and play started shortly after 2 p.m. The last couple finished about 4.30. Having had a hasty tea at Henbury Hill House, they were driven to Bristol station for the 5.15."

The recording of all events was meticulous. On one never-to-be-forgotten occasion "The Gentlemen went up by the 10.20 from Clifton Down to Stinchcombe and played a return match against Stinchcombe Hill Golf Club Second team, resulting in an easy victory for the home team by 22 holes.

"This result was no doubt owing largely to the fact that the match was played in thick fog, and also that we were unable to play our strongest team (Major Archdale was unable to go at the last minute owing to illness).

"Lunch was kindly provided after the first round and our team returned by the 5.37. A break was kindly put at our disposal to drive our team to and from the bottom of Stinchcombe Hill and Berkeley Road Station."

Henbury greens and tees were still a mess, and the only thing to do was move them where possible and try to improve matters in any way practicable. It was a relief when tee boxes were provided for sand because, it must be remembered, the modern technological development of the tee peg had not yet happened. The ball was teed on a little squid of damp sand taken from the box between thumb and the first two fingers and pressed into a pyramid on the grass on which the ball would be delicately placed for the drive. The scattering of sand in striking the ball had a good cumulative effect on the quality of the grass on the tees.

Woe betide anyone who dumped rubbish in the tee box in those days and for a long time to come. Boxes were well

21

made, of decent, seasoned wood, varnished against the weather, and with rope handles. Henbury had some particularly good ones, the writer can recall. Their proper use persisted even after World War Two, but the wooden peg had swamped the market and slowly sand disappeared.

Wooden boxes were often stolen for firewood or possible garden use, but the metal ones were weighted with concrete to discourage bored youths from throwing them into the trees or the Trym for no other reason than to be a nuisance.

The club now had a real identity and place in the community. Members broke off the competitive action for a swinging dance at the Salutation Inn, and 94 attended with tickets at 7s.6d. each. Dancing started at nine o'clock to the music of G. Webb's Four, and Southwood (?) provided supper.

Phyllis Lobbett with a first-class caddie of the times.

---

*Footnote*: Question of the new Licensing Law as regards the club was discussed and the opinion of Mr Marshall Hall K.C. was read by the secretary. Decided. . .it was necessary to have an attendant permanently in the clubhouse during play hours, who would have entire charge of the refreshments (January 3, 1903).

# Riding By

Arthur Baker had lived for years at Henbury Hill House, and knew everyone. He was familiar with every stick and stone on Coombe Hill and the surrounding countryside, and he had an idea for the expansion of the golf course.

Imagine him riding his horse down Sandy Lane, the track on the right of our ninth fairway, on his way to the village and on to his offices in Redcliff. Those fields over the hedge on his right, sloping down from the woods to the Trym, encompassed by hedges and walls, would serve us well, he would muse. He had doubtless talked it over with his old friend Robinson who knew the place just as well. They were men of action, but also men of vision.

Baker called a general meeting of club members for six o'clock on the evening of Friday, May 11, 1894, at his house. As it turned out he did not get there in time, and Robinson took the chair until his arrival. All the committee and a large number of members were there, and Baker eventually put forward his plan.

"We can take the golf course down to the southern slopes of Coombe Hill, lease the two fields and go across the Trym to Canford Lane," he told them.

The vote was unanimous. The two inside fields were to be rented from Mr Cooper at £15 per annum. Cooper? Mr Cooper, indeed.

Extra hut accommodation was to come from money raised by members' subscriptions, "or in any way the committee may see fit." The new hut would be for the ladies, and the space between the two buildings would be roofed over.

The estimates were similar to those for the original hut, and a small pavilion was also considered, but Robinson, Edgar Baker, son of Arthur, and Hiatt Baker, who had been appointed to handle the business, decided it would be better and cheaper to have a bigger house altogether.

Eventually they considered rough plans and estimates from three Westbury builders. F. Williams tendered £89 5s.,

W. Wellbridge, £68, and H.W. Harris reckoned £64 10s. Harris, of course, got the job. He lived in the first house up from the police station.

Edgar Baker, who was also hon secretary at the time, took Harris's plan to a Park Street architect named Wood who strongly recommended a number of alterations. Harris, knowing a good thing when he saw it, had no hesitation in agreeing to these. He would build for £82 10s., he said. What is more, he offered the club about twenty loads of earth for levelling, and building grass bunkers.

The fields were to be taken over in the middle of August, and in the meantime Harris got on with the job, contentedly agreeing with such last minute thoughts as the tarring over of the new roof under the tiles.

Members promised £22 towards the cost of the new building, but, Edgar Baker announced sorrowfully, "Several have not replied to the appeal". Because of this it was agreed that any minus balance should be borrowed on interest not exceeding five per cent, as much as possible to be paid back annually together with the interest.

It was September 15th when Wood the architect proposed his changes, and by October 16th the work was done. It was then thought it would be a good idea to have some kind of railings or fencing around the new clubhouse at a cost of no more than £8, and Harris was our man. The secretary went off to buy "tables, forms, washstands, etc . . ." The clubhouse and fittings cost £119 8s. 6d. A voluntary subscription was raised, and £37 7s. was given or promised, but a debit of £45 remained.

Saturday, October 27th, was Opening Day for the clubhouse, and the new course, for the work had been going along well outside, – and it rained! An even sadder fact was that only about thirty members turned up.

What the absentees missed was tea, as much bread and butter as one wished, and cake, all for sixpence a head. A Mrs Thompson, of Botany Bay, Henbury, – was this a public house? – was engaged to supervise the tea and to wash up afterwards. This was to be a standing Saturday arrangement with Mrs T. at 1s.6d. a time with her own tea thrown in. The secretary had to lay on all the supplies each week. Every Saturday a boy was engaged at sixpence to bring up water from the village, and attend to the clubhouse, sweep out and tidy up generally.

This was the start of the wooden pavilion that was to last down the years, with various additions and improvements from time to time. It stood on the site of the putting green in front of our clubhouse, and in time it had a fine, large putting green of its own, stretching almost to our eleventh tee but completely surrounded by a privet hedge.

Memories come flooding of moments in social life in that old clubhouse. The men's holy of holies contained the only bar. The central lounge and tea room was for mixed members, but otherwise segregation of the sexes was complete; no lady could set foot over the threshold of the men's lounge and bar.

The procedure for the parched golfer to obtain a drink in the central room was to press a buzzer at a small hatch which opened upwards like a rabbit hutch behind the bar. Sometimes it was better to bang on the woodwork. This would eventually fly up and a disembodied voice betraying the strain of service would growl against a background of men's hollering and guffawing: "Yes?"

"Ah, a pint of bitter please, and a . . ." Crash! Hatch down.

Hatch up. A hand would poke a pint through. "Anythin' else?"

"Gin and tonic, and . . ." Crash! Hatch down. A chocolate bar or a packet of biscuits would be worth a couple of crashes, and the final presentation of change would bring the trap down like a guillotine.

Yet the author and a handful of others will always remember the old place with affection. It was accidentally burnt down in 1959 even as the present building was completed, and you cannot have better timing than that!

---

*Footnote*: Christmas Eve, Monday, December 24th 1894, a bogey competition was played. "Weather beautifully fine and warm. Only eight gentlemen put in an appearance, and no ladies." Scores: 1, Major Archdale 2 down; 2, H.P. Luckman, 3 down.

Golf clubs, Balls and Requisites by best English and Scottish makers. Gigantic stock of everything for the game – Harris's. First established City Golf Depot, St Stephen's Street.

# Big Hitting

A shot of 159 yards won the long driving contest set up for Easter Monday in 1894, and it settled many a dispute.

The distance was measured to the point where the ball first touched the ground, and that is very different from measuring to where the ball finishes. A carry of 159 yards with 1894 equipment and a Silvertown Best was something special.

Each contestant had three shots, taken consecutively or otherwise, the balls having to pitch within lines 50 yards apart. Many gentlemen performed, and Vincent Fedden and R. Deane did pretty well, but Walter Jefferis, off nine, one of the two lowest handicaps in the club, produced the best effort to win.

The driving started at 11.00 and afterwards everyone moved to the first green for a putting competition. Putts were taken from four, six, eight and ten yards, the ball being placed at any point at those distances but never putted twice down the same line. Three tries were allowed at each distance, each holed ball counting two and a ball within six inches counting one. And who should win but Jefferis again, with Bertram Matthews second.

The two Arthurs – Baker and Robinson – gave a cup for that afternoon's handicap, and this was the Arthur Cup we play for today. They called it the Arthur Cup then, but the two men gave several other trophies at different times and it is sometimes confusing in later documentation to distinguish which was which. The Arthur Cup at one time seemed to become the President's Cup, but for the moment we will deal with the original design and title.

The outcome must have been a shock because Elfreda Baker with a handicap of 45, waltzed away with it by six strokes with 71 nett. Her rounds were 59 and 57. Abigail Way was runner-up with 77, followed by the Misses G. and A. Baker. The first man among the 21 entries was Matthews with 140-56-84. There was no gross prize, but H.P. Luckman, a Clifton College master, and Deane, led with 101, with Miss Way only one behind.

Men and women played against each other in the same competitions without favour, and there was a great deal of activity with handicaps and regular matches.

For instance, when Miss M. Miles won the March bogey after a tie at five down with Miss A. Deane, seven of her 13 rivals were men. Two rounds were played, and Miss Miles, off 13, was two down the first time round and three the next. "By the Rules," which must have meant some sort of countback, "Miss Miles was declared winner."

The hut was kept locked when members went out to play, but one afternoon someone left a key in the lock. Along came one of the Westbury village boys who whipped out the key and disappeared from the scene. He came back with a companion that evening. They took some balls, and cash out of the lemonade moneybox, which they broke open. They were caught, and both names are in the logbook. Whether summary justice was meted out is not known, but it was decided not to prosecute.

* * *

Pressure had been mounting all that year for something to be done about better and larger accommodation because men and women had no room to themselves, and to say there was overcrowding was to put it mildly. Another cause for concern was lack of space on the course.

In March Walter Jefferis entertained a Handicap committee in his offices, and they came away full of ideas for stretching and improving the holes on Coombe Hill, but there was also the glimmering of another scheme.

It was decided to elect Cooper, son of Mr F. Cooper, of Westbury, an honorary member of the club. Why? No reason is recorded, but Cooper must have been the man referred to in the treasurer's earlier report. The name was to crop up again very soon in a way that makes it obvious the interests of Henbury golfers were in the hands of some very astute characters indeed.

*Footnote*: President's Cup (Saturday, May 12th): W.H. Jefferis 91-13-78. Net, or money prize, divided by Mrs H. Matthews, 141-65-76, and Miss G. Baker, 111-35-76.

Whit Monday (May 14th). Warm and no wind. A bogey competition was held. Scores: C.B. Lee Warner – a new name – handicap 11, even; B.H. Matthews (ten) 3 down.

# "Pay Up, Please!"

A severe winter followed by a very dry summer wreaked havoc on the greens in 1895. (Incidentally, the flooding in the Avon that November was the greatest ever known.)

The accounts showed a net gain of £24 18. 3½., "making with last year's balance a total credit of £39 13s. 2d., and of this the committee propose to apply £38 1s. 6d. towards the liquidation of the debt on the clubhouse".

The financial result was "extremely satisfactory," and "it is hoped with an increased number of members that the necessarily increased expenditure will be easily provided for". Then came a plea that those members who had not subscribed would do so, and that those who had would increase their subscriptions to wipe off the balance.

It was a considerable loss to the club's administration when Bertram Matthews and Miss M. Miles resigned as respective hon secretaries, and their absences were felt in the teams as well. Both had left the area. Walter Jefferis and Miss Agnes Harford were elected.

A year later the Greens committee were still complaining that if only they could spend more on the course still greater improvements could be made.

A rule had been laid down that "The Green committee shall have full power to lay down, alter, as required, keep in order and repair the links (including the pavilion), and for such purposes may expend money to the amount of £5.0.0.". This grave responsibility lay on the shoulders of Major Archdale, Edgar Baker, Jefferis and Matthews.

Accounts were almost a carbon copy of the previous statement – "A nett gain of £28.4.4. making, together with the balance brought forward . . . a total credit balance of £30.7.6. Of this the committee propose to apply £29.2.0. towards liquidation of the debt on the clubhouse, leaving a debt of £10 still outstanding."

If they could see the debt cleared, said the committee, they felt they could carry out "various little matters which

*Above*, The Archdale Inkstand.

*Treasurer's Account 1893*

| Receipts | £ | s. | d | | Expenditure | £ | s. | d |
|---|---|---|---|---|---|---|---|---|
| Balance in Hand | 3 | 7 | 10½ | | Coats | 18 | 4 | 0 |
| Subscriptions | 45 | 2 | 6 | | Sec Expenses | 1 | 9 | 8½ |
| 14 keys | 0 | 14 | 0 | | Printing | 1 | 1 | 6 |
| 14 lockers | 3 | 10 | 0 | | Pencil | 0 | 0 | 6 |
| Visitors | 3 | 0 | 0 | | Caddies Badges | 0 | 5 | 0 |
| Ginger beer | 1 | 14 | 5 | | 2 doz. Keys | 1 | 0 | 0 |
| Balls | 0 | 11 | 0 | | Lockers | 5 | 1 | 1 |
| Handicaps | 0 | 11 | 3 | | Rent | 10 | 0 | 0 |
| Mr Crawford | 6 | 10 | 6 | | Mr Davies | 1 | 5 | 0 |
| | £59 | 1 | 6¾ | | Flags | 1 | 9 | 6 |
| Expenditure | £44 | 6 | 8½ | | 12 Tumblers | 0 | 3 | 0 |
| | 14 | 14 | 10¼ | | Rent of House etc | 0 | 1 | 3 |
| | | | | | Bennett | 0 | 7 | 9 |
| | | | | | Oxtons | 0 | 1 | 0 |
| | | | | | Lambert | 0 | 2 | 6 |
| Balance in Hand £14 . 14 | | | 10¼ | | Score Cards | 0 | 17 | 0 |
| | | | | | Ginger beer | 1 | 18 | 0 |
| | | | | | Lawn Smith | 0 | 8 | 2 |
| | | | | | Blacksmith for sticks etc | 1 | 11 | 6 |
| | | | | | Meter | 0 | 11 | 6 |
| | | | | | Lockings, Tea | 0 | 2 | 6 |
| | | | | | C. | £44 | 6 | 8½ |

---

*Footnote:* Hunter and Vaughan, Broad Street. Golfers – note prices: The Defiance, best 1s. ball on the market. Climax, 15s.6d. doz. Spark 18s. doz.

would be to the improvement of the club".

The leading players were Horace Pope Luckman who was one of the first masters of Clifton College. He was a house tutor in the new junior school and a games organiser. He was house master of the South Town prep school from 1880 until 1898 when he died.

The Arthur Challenge Cup had developed into a four rounds tournament, and Luckman won it with scratch scores in a good descending order of 57, 56, 54 and 53, two shots better than B.H. Matthews, who had the best nett.

Jefferis was consistently good, and Archdale, who rarely lost a match, produced the lowest scratch score in a club competition with an 86 in a December medal. The gallant major will always be remembered for presenting the ladies with the Archdale Inkstand for competition, a splendid trophy that is sadly under-valued today, being given no more than the competitive significance of a high handicap medal. How much more suitable as a major trophy!

A review of 1895 said that "with regard to club matches the gentlemen have not been very successful, having played twelve, won four and lost eight, but in connection with this your committee would remark that our opponents' teams have been far stronger than heretofore. The ladies have been more successful, in spite of the fact that they have not once been able to put their full strength into the field, having played five, won three and lost two."

A record of 37 for the gentlemen's course was returned by H.E. Lee, a new member who quickly found himself playing top in team matches.

In September Major Archdale retired from the committee, Matthews was back and Jefferis was leaving Bristol. At the sixth annual meeting, held in the clubhouse for the first time, it was decided to split the secretary's general duties with a match secretary. Matthews was elected hon secretary, and A.C. Livingstone Learmonth the new match secretary.

Only eight people attended the meeting because of the cold, and there was no heat in the building. In fact two more years were to pass before anything was done about getting a stove for the place.

Henbury had put forward the idea of a united golf dance somewhere in Clifton, asking Bristol & Clifton, Backwell, Long Ashton, the Downs and Portishead if they would co-operate, but Bristol & Clifton "could not see their way to this," and the idea was shelved until the following Easter.

# Club Colours

The idea of club colours had been raised some weeks earlier and referred to the ladies' committee. On March 20th, 1897, it was revealed that primrose and hunting red had been chosen.

A year later the following letter was received from J.M. Stevens, Hatters, Hosiers and Shirt Tailors, of 52 Park Street, Bristol. –

Sir,
    As you know the members of your golf club will not wear the ribbon because it is like the MCC. I was suggesting to Miss Baker the advisability of changing it and rearrange the colours somewhat like the enclosed bit. I have about 18 yards of the other left on hand and if you would take up a new one and allow me to charge 3d a yard extra for it, it would soon pay for the piece I have (that is if it was worn as it ought to be). Miss Baker said I had better write to you.
        Yours obediently,
          J.M. Stevens.
P.S. – I should think a ribbon ¾ in. narrower would be better for the ladies. I have roughly sketched a design which would be quite unique. It could be modified. February 3rd, 1898.

Nobody knows what happened after that.
On September 4th, 1897, the committee received a letter from Miss A.T. Fry. –

The ladies in the club could, I think, be induced to play more if they had some prizes to play for. Lamentable admission, but true! Mrs Davis of Minchinhampton told me of a very good scheme that she had devised. She got every lady in the club to subscribe one shilling, to which I think no one will object, and with the money she got a set of twelve silver spoons and they played for one every month. I think if we could do the same at Henbury it would be an excellent thing.

Miss Fry got her way, and the first spoon was played for on November 3rd and won by Mrs Langley (12) with a nett 93. Miss Fry won hers in December with one up against bogey.

The January of 1898 was too cold for a clubhouse meeting, and Arthur Baker took the chair in his own house. There was some hitch over fire insurance for a stove at the club, and it was decided to leave the matter until next season.

Secretary Matthews said the conditions of insuring the clubhouse against burglary at a premium of 10s.6d. were not clearly understood. He was asked to get a blank policy for the president to peruse "and then to follow out his instructions regarding same".

Later in the year it was decided to add an extra room, half as a place to keep the tea and ginger beer, and half as an outhouse where the wheelbarrow etc could be kept. As ever, Mr Harris would do this for £9.5.0. and was told to carry on.

---

*Footnote*: Towards the end of the 1890s there were nearly 300 golfers in Bristol, most of whom played on the Downs. F.H. Thomas, a prominent member of Henbury 25 years later, was for many years secretary of the Downs club.

# Loafers

Village boys were making themselves a nuisance hanging about on the course, scrounging and thrashing the furze about to find balls to try and sell them back to members. Arthur Baker called them "loafers" and demanded action. "It will be a good thing to get a policeman up here," he told Matthews. "He could come up for a short time on Saturday afternoons and reprimand any boys found loafing about."

Badges for caddies had still not arrived, but when they did Baker said he would give them to a few boys thought good enough to be first class caddies. It was for Matthews and Pople, the professional, to decide their fitness for the job. Pople was told not to play on Saturday afternoons but stay in his hut and look after the boys. Keep an eye on them, he was instructed, because caddies would be encouraged to steal more balls if members bought any from them.

All balls, it was suggested, should be sold to Pople who was to retail them to members. Furthermore, all caddies, as far as possible, were to be engaged through Pople, and he was to have an assistant.

The club had grown considerably by 1898, and the number of visitors was surprisingly increased. The latter fact prompted a further instruction to Pople that all visitors' names should be entered in the Visitors' Book, which was to be put in a much more prominent position. But no one knows where that was . . .

People who moved off the defined pathways across the course, which were the same then as they are now, were straying about and causing another problem. A large notice board was to be made calling pedestrians' attention to the fact that the Hill was rented by the golf club. Strangers were requested to keep to the footpaths.

The balance at the end of that year was £46.13.11. After providing for all liabilities there was £28.13.11. clear, and a stock of balls and clubs in hand worth £15.

The clubhouse was free of debt, and a number of new lockers had been provided. Membership was going up all the time, and the club was prospering. Sixty members had now joined from outside, and it was proposed to increase their ranks by ten. All this meant more money could be spent on the course.

Sometime between 1899 and 1903 Matthews relinquished the post of secretary, and once again Edgar Baker stepped into the breach. A year later the hon secretary was one Harry Buchanan who did the job until 1908 and was then elected hon treasurer. His place was taken by Harry Andrews who was quite a player with the amateur record of 34 for nine holes to his credit, and he stayed in office until the fateful year of 1914.

* * *

Detective work in the basement of Bristol Reference Library among tattered and dusty old newspapers that have not yet been micro-filmed has its drawbacks, not least the need to retreat every two hours to replenish the parking meter.

The first setback was the loss through misplacement, misappropriation or misadventure of the relevant papers for 1891. A hopeful search of *The Times* revealed nothing more than the information that on December 10th Gladstone had made a thunderous speech on Rural Reform. Other headlines proclaimed Fighting On The Indian Frontier and Arab Uprising In Central Africa.

One interesting fact emerged. As the intrepid band of golfers met at the Vicarage that first evening "nearly all the leading inhabitants of Westbury-on-Trym met for entertainment in the Hall in aid of Boys' School funds".

A gentleman of the *Bristol Evening News* staff who wrote about golf from the early part of this century, and who called himself by the prosaic name of "Bunker", yielded a great deal of priceless information about the whole area.

Much more may have been gleaned had it not been for the depredations of a razor-wielding vandal who, in the name of research, has removed whole pages of the paper, year after year, to make a collection of Bunker's articles, or possibly the angling notes. For what is left we must be grateful . . .

---

*Footnote*: Golfers – remember that year-old Golf balls can be made as good as new for 9d. and 1s. each – Capern's Golf Ball Co., Portland Square, Bristol.

# £180 Rent

Details of a Henbury lease dated November 13th, 1906, come to light among the confusing early deeds, and give the first inkling of the financial arrangements on behalf of the club.

John Charles Harford, of Falcondale, Lampeter, county of Cardigan, being the lessor, agreed: to let the whole course (18 holes) for 21 years at a rent of £180 to September 29, 1916, and £200 for the rest of the term; reserved right to dispose of land abutting on Canford Lane for a depth of 110 feet, the rest to be abated at the rate of £4 per acre; to extend the existing quarry on Coombe Hill; to construct any bunkers or obstacles for the purpose of golf, and cut down or root out hedges, bushes or gorse, but undertook to replace any if required; to sub-let land to Frederick Augustine Cooper, of Court Farm, Westbury-on-Trym.*

The signatories were Arthur Baker, Henbury Hill House, merchant; Herbert Midelton Baker, of The Holmes, Stoke Bishop, merchant; William Charles Beloe, Canynge Road, Clifton, merchant; Bertram Henry Matthews, of Shirehampton, printer; Arthur Robinson, of Lawrence Weston, merchant; Henry Holden Townsend, of Stoke Bishop, chemist; Fitz Sampson Way, The Manor House, Henbury, Major (R.M.) ret; William Windus, Downfield Road, Clifton, company director; Hampden Vincent Barnard, Cecil Lodge, Sneyd Park, corn broker.

This appeared over the signatures of A. Ernest Ashmead, of Chain House, Eastfield, a chartered accountant of Hudson Smith Briggs and Co., Exchange Chambers, Bristol, and Col. P. Burges, land agent, of 11, Marsh Street, Bristol.

---

* It was clear at last that our Mr. Cooper farmed Westbury Court Farm, where the Westbury Post Office stands. And his son, who was made an honorary member, was manager of the National Provincial Bank in the village and lived at 6, Southfield Road. And his son is Joseph Cooper, the famous pianist.

# Remarkable Man

Arthur Baker died suddenly at the age of 67 on February 22, 1909, a fortnight after presiding at the annual meeting.

By any standards he was a remarkable man, and there is no doubt he was guide and mentor to the golf club. He was born in Bristol and educated at Bristol Grammar School, leaving at 16 to go straight into his father's business (William Baker and Sons, Redcliff Backs). Nine years later Arthur was a partner. He had also joined the 1st Gloucester Volunteer Rifles.

From 1874 when he represented Redcliff ward on the City Council, he enjoyed a long spell in Bristol politics and was chairman of Bristol South Conservative Association. He was also made a justice of the peace in 1874, and became High Sheriff of Bristol in 1892. He was admitted to the Society of Merchant Venturers in 1869 and held innumerable offices.

Two years before Baker formed the golf club, Bakers Ltd amalgamated with Spillers of Cardiff, and he became a director of the largest milling and trading corn business in the country, with offices and mills in Cardiff and Newcastle as well as Bristol. It seems almost certain that his pre-knowledge of golf derived from his journeys up and down the country.

That February meeting was a success. There were then 250 members, and it was decided to increase subscriptions to £3.3.0. for men and £1.11.6. for ladies. An entrance fee of £3.3.0. was approved, and for five-day members £2.2.0. and £1.5.0. fees were decided.

All the officers were re-elected together with Walter Windus, of Downfield Place, Clifton, as an additional vice-president. He had joined the club with his wife in 1897, and in 1902 he was president of Rodway Hill! They moved around a lot in those days. A.L. Purnell, of Clyde Lodge, Westbury – mark the name well – and Miss E. Hemingway, of Downleaze, were elected to two vacancies on the committee.

Members at the 1922 Christmas meeting.

By this time Henbury had acquired considerable status, and Baker was thrilled to announce that in all probability the championship of the Gloucestershire Golf Union would be held here in 1910.

It is not known how long George Talbot Plum had been a member but he was one of the best known of Westbury personalities. That February, Plum was appointed assistant hon secretary to the Gloucestershire Union. It was rather amusing that just after this announcement Henbury second team, assisted by Harry Andrews and Arthur Purnell – second team? – went to Alveston and won by the odd point. And who should be on the Alveston team but Talbot Plum!

Purnell was picked to play for Gloucestershire against Worcestershire, but beyond the fact that they were thrashed nothing is known of the play. Purnell was Henbury's first playing ambassador, and he was useful. He won the March medal with 77-2-75, and his gross was better than any other nett score.

In springtime our friend Bunker reported that "Henbury professional John Pople is lying seriously ill with an attack of rheumatic fever. All golfers will wish him a speedy recovery". His job was taken in the meantime by W.J. Hearne, an assistant from Bristol & Clifton "through the courtesy of Reid, the Failand professional".

Playing with Captain Guy Baker, Hearne went round Henbury in 68 to equal Pople's record. Here is the card: Bogey, out: 4 4 3 5 5 4 5 4 5 = 39; in, 3 4 4 5 5 5 3 5 4 = 38. Hearne, out: 4 4 3 5 4 3 3 3 5 = 34; in, 4 3 4 4 4 3 4 4 = 34. The writer admits he cannot make head or tail of the order of play in this instance. There are changes in holes of which we have no knowledge.

Reporting Hearne's score, Bunker said: "Pople did two 68s last year, but the course was somewhat easier then." It sounded like sour grapes.

Fortunately Pople recovered well and was back in action in the beginning of June when he went to Shirehampton and shot 69, six better than bogey. A couple of days later, playing with Dr. Kyle, Pople recovered the Henbury record with 66, with an astonishing run of 4 2 3 4 5 3 3 3 4, a total of 31 for the first half, and returned in 35 with 4 3 3 4 5 4 4 4 4.

A final comment from Bunker on a glorious summer in 1909 concerns Purnell who scored 72 in one medal and followed with 70 in the next: "It will be interesting to hear what the Henbury Handicap committee will do with Mr Purnell."

# What to Wear

The problem of what to wear caused a great deal of concern in the hot summer of 1911. "The knickerbocker suit seems to be the favourite but this, with the thick stockings, is very hot in the weather we have been experiencing," Bunker wrote. "Cricketing suits are very popular this summer, but on some links players have been seen without coats. I am glad to say as far as this district is concerned they have been few and far between."

He also aired his views about Henbury. His *Evening News* column of May 29th contained the following: "The Gloucestershire championship is due at Henbury on June 14th. At the present time the lower part of the course is not in ideal condition. The cut fairway is too narrow, and the daisies are not kept under, but, no doubt, as there is plenty of time, the matter will have the attention of the Henbury committee. It is a privilege to have the championship held on a Bristol course and everything will doubtless be done to make the meeting a great success."

There was a record entry of 80 for the sixth county championship two weeks later, and our correspondent was there. "On account of drought the ground was very hard and the greens on the top part of the course very fiery, but the committee spared no effort to make conditions as good as possible."

The championship was won in startling fashion by George Grieve, of Cotswold Hills, who scored a fine 70 in the morning and followed with 77 to go 13 shots clear. The Cheltenham club won the team championship with 251, and Henbury came seventh, only eight shots behind. Purnell scored 85, H.J. Andrews 86, H.C. Chetwood-Aitken, 88, and the Rev R.L. Whytehead, 89.

Perhaps the daisies were not kept under too well, but it is sad to relate that the championship did not return to Henbury for another 68 years – in 1979.

# Of Course . . .

The first two fairways were turned into a wheatfield during the Great War, and the lower part of the course was returned to farm use. Cattle and sheep moved in. Golf was confined to the remaining top holes.

Restoration took a long time, and it was not until May 29th, 1920, that a new 18 holes course was opened. It was said to be in excellent condition, but another severe dry spell in August put members back on temporary greens.

The course was considerably lengthened in the next twelve months "which the members greatly appreciated".

The enjoyable matches of pre-war days with Rodway Hill were resumed. Dr. A.G. Morris played top for Henbury, "but Rodway normally won because they were one of the strongest clubs in the district". Sunday play started on August 15th, 1920.

On May 6th, 1922, after spending £1,000, Henbury celebrated "the opening of the course at full length, the permanent putting greens being brought into use. All was in good order, and some low scores were returned." However, the best seems to have been 95-24-71 by B.F. Williams who played exactly to his handicap.

After all this development the club still came up with a profit of £120.

Prominent among the members were S. Becket Hurst, who was captain six years later, H.L. Leonard, Ernest Richard Smale, also to be captain, and Waldo Thomas. The name of Cavell was to appear with great regularity in the years ahead with Arthur the father and W.H. and W.D.S. the sons. W.H. Cavell was captain that year in the steps of his father who held office for the first two years of peace.

Harold Faraday Proctor was a leading figure, and it was he who led the "outsiders" in a match of 26 a side against the "insiders," a team of club members resident in the parish of Westbury and captained by architect R.C. James of Grange Court Road. Faraday Proctor's team won 20–15, but the arithmetic after singles and foursomes is perhaps a little baffling.

Among the many who were to become influential in the club's future were H.S. 'Bertie' Young and Frank Davis, later to be chairman and secretary respectively, and Frank Preston, one of the best liked of men who was then secretary and who contributed greatly to local golf with a newspaper column. It is the writer's fervent hope that he got paid for it!

More money went on the course in 1923, some £300 on bunkering, and great care was lavished on the greens. The ground staff (numbers unknown) had a new triple lawn mower, and several other machines and necessary equipment.

The kitchen was extended, and the clubhouse repainted outside. The horses were given a new shelter, and a start was made on "building a road for motors to the Club House and accommodation to park motors". There followed "a much needed extension to the gentlemen's quarters".

Progressive work continued, and the course began to settle and mature. Revenue fell in 1924, partly because of a wet season, and the year showed a loss of £204 15s. 9d.

Gradual scrapping of the hedges and dismantling of walls had given Henbury a broader aspect. It became necessary to tighten up the greens, and the bunkering programme was intensified. There was "plenty of scope for improving this most popular of courses," Preston explained.

"Apart from the low subscription required by the Bristol clubs it is very inexpensive to reach the various courses," Bunker wrote in the *Evening News* of November 12th. "Henbury is one of the easiest if one is lucky enough to catch the Brentry bus at the Westbury Tram Terminus. It then takes only two or three minutes. There is a short cut through the fields for pedestrians."

---

*Footnote*: In June 1924 Mrs Waldo Thomas, playing with Mr James King, holed a brassie shot for an eagle two at the third (236 yards, par four). "Only once has this hole been secured in two – by Harry Fisher, the greenkeeper. Fisher is a long hitter." This hole is our eleventh.

# Of Gorse . . .

George Prescott is now 81, which makes him only twenty years younger than the club.

He was born in Westbury, and has played golf on the hill for more than seventy years. To get home after a game he and his friends used to play shots down over the course and across the fields to Pratt's Garage in the village. Remember, there was no Falcondale Road, and hardly a house in sight.

In 1900 the *Golfing Annual* referred to Henbury as "a course of nine holes, varying in length from 135 yards to 360 yards (par 35). There is also a ladies' course of nine holes from 125 yards to 320, the par of which (for ladies) is 35".

This was confusing. All golf activity was confined to Coombe Hill, and the holes were laid out with almost the same design as today but in a different order. There must have been an overlap, but nowhere is this explained. The best way to understand the lay-out is for the writer to refer to "our holes" (as they are in 1991) in conjunction with the numbers of a hundred years ago.

Easier still is the mental exercise of following George Prescott and his Boswell, Bill Rangecroft, on a stroll round the course. Rangecroft, an enthusiastic and knowledgeable golfer, author some years ago of a helpful *Short History of Henbury Golf Club*, made a tape recording of Prescott's reminiscences as they walked and talked their way round.

The first two holes were much shorter long ago, but always followed the same paths, although the second was a little straighter. For a short experimental period in the middle years they were played as the 17th and 18th. They make a fine finish, but it was not a popular effort. The first tee was the one we all use in the winter, opposite the clubhouse. A subsequent shot sliced over the hedge ended in the farmyard where Hyland Grove stands. The hedge ran back across the top of the fairway of our tenth, just where the fairway starts as you come up the hill.

The second tee was further over, near a pond on the baseline of our practice ground. There was a beech copse in that corner of the driveway, and a thick hedge ran all along the player's right to the clubhouse. No such thing as a practice area existed either on the ground or in the thoughts of men. Nothing separated the holes except rough grass and the odd bush. Bunkers were grass, and the trees were planted after World War Two.

Our eleventh was the third, a bogey four and virtually the same length as today. The trees separating it from the 18th, and the shrubbery in front of the tees are the product of recent times. However, there was a pond on the left just about where the fairway starts and level with the back of the tiger tee of the first hole.

The ponds scattered about Coombe Hill were expressly watering holes for cattle and sheep and in no way formed golfing hazards, except possibly the last one.

As the player came off that green the path led to the fourth tee – our 14th – and a hole much shorter than today, but still a bogey five.

In front of the tee, stretching as far as the beech on the left, was a sea of gorse. The ladies had their forward tee, but the gorse had to be carried with the drive. The green was in the region of the left hillock at the gap. Later, as the quarry was extended, the green now in disuse but maintained as a turf nursery, was constructed, and the hole reduced to a four.

The quarry, which played such an important part in Henbury's history, was an awesome piece of commercial development. When its time had run out it was as deep as the drop from the Suspension Bridge to the water. It was a chasm on the right side of the drive, nearly 150 yards long and 100 yards across to Blaise Woods. It is inconceivable to those who have come to the club since the new holes were made over the top of it.

The only time it was likely for a ball to be knocked into the quarry was from a 'thinned' bunker recovery from short of the green. Any ball hit into the depths, providing it missed one of the workers, would still be bouncing if the place had not been filled in, a job that took seven years to complete.

Gorse also made our 15th and 16th quite spectacular. There were pathways through it, but the carries were formidable and at the same time exciting.

Considering the present day reactions to the bushes in front of our eleventh, one can imagine the hullabaloo if the gorse remained today. Yet there was never a mention until the decision to uproot it all. "It looked quite nice, you know!" said George.

George Prescott.

---

*Footnote*: By the courtesy of the Porthcawl Golf Club a team went down on Saturday, April 2nd, and played in a mixed foursome match in the afternoon, resulting in a win for Henbury by three holes (1898).

D.F. Harris in one at the seventh (130 yards) – our 13th. It was thought this was the first time it had been done, but W.H. Rowlands, the Gloucestershire county cricket captain, did it some time earlier (1927).

# Birdies Galore

Pheasant and partridge abounded on Coombe Hill, and all belonged to the Harford estate. Two gamekeepers were employed, and shooting parties were held "for the gentry". "They didn't shoot on the course," said George. "My dad used to get the odd pheasant for Sunday dinner," he grinned, but did not enlarge on the subject.

Sometimes wormcasts were so bad on these holes that play was impossible, but after drastic treatment matters improved ever after. For years there was trouble with our 15th green. Our 16th was the sixth, much the same outline as now, but near the tee there stood a magnificent beech. Its stump is still visible. The red maple now flourishes in its stead. Our 13th was the seventh, played from the very front tee at about 120 yards. There was no cross bunker, but grass traps guarded both sides of the green. So to the Devil's Ladder – our 12th and their eighth – so-called because of the steep path behind the green that ran down to Coombe Dingle. There is an old tee forward of any other at our 12th, and that was the one used. Behind it ran a fence and wire over from the back of the eleventh green to the back of the 14th tee. The green had a steep slope up from front to back, and many a ball has run off the green towards the player. There was no bank at the back of the green, and any shot hit too far was in danger of ending up in Coombe Dingle as well.

Our short 17th was the ninth, known as Oak Tree on the card, but the magnificent reason for the name was brought down by lightning. The hole is not changed much, grass bunkers, of course, and the cross bunker is "recent".

The next was played from the ladies' front tee over a five-foot hedge running across the top of the fairway from the back of the eleventh. "There was a gap and you went through or over it," said George Prescott.

The woods on the right were full of pheasants. The green was shaped like a basin, and any second shot landing on it was almost certain to gather in the bottom and give a birdie putt. This was the limit of the course before the lower part was developed. The riddle remains: How did they get two courses out of these ten holes?

E.R. (Ted) Raymond gave this photograph to the club (4.10.'79). It portrays Mrs Cissie Mortimer (fifth from left, front row) who was stewardess for seven years from 1914, and was taken in the early stages of the Great War. Next to her are her staff, Blanche and a Mrs C ____. The men in the front row are members, and, standing, are nearly all professionals and ground staff, including Jack Branch and Fisher.

# Downstairs

The Drop Hole was constructed to switch play "downstairs" to the lower course. The player walked off the tenth green (our 18th) to a tee on the right where a clump of bushes and small trees now stand. The green was directly below, between the woods, and its outline is still visible. Our pathway from the third tee along to the fairway was actually the ledge above the green. The back of the green was steeply banked to stop balls going over on to our fifth fairway, and the drop that side was more than six feet.

Go on to our forward third tee for their twelfth, and drive back over the green you have just left. It was a shot of little more than 200 yards to a green short of the ridge where a decent drive finishes now. But the ridge was then a hedge and the boundary of the course.

After World War Two the Drop hole was abandoned with the purchase of Cherry Orchard, the hedge disappeared and our present third and fourth were constructed.

Now we walk down behind our fifth tee to the Trym Hole. Bill Rangecroft describes it:

This was the 13th, which may account for so many golfers meeting disaster here. The hole was called the Windmill, and in fact a mill stood on the ground beyond the Trym, just over the steel grid bridge.

Before 1914 the green was further up the hill to the right of the windmill on land now occupied by gardens of houses fronting on to Canford Lane. The tee was on the site of the ladies' abandoned forward tee.

The steel grid is a recent addition to replace a wooden bridge washed away in a storm. That bridge stood in front of the green. The stone bridge beyond the present seventh green is very ancient. It is to be hoped the latter bridge will be preserved as time goes by.

The next hole – our eighth and their 14th – has seen considerable change. When the windmill and the original 13th green were in existence the next tee was to the left of that green. The drive was downhill over the land behind the present seventh green on to what is now the eighth fairway beyond the ridge.

A hedge across the fairway at that point, where the ridge is, enclosed a paddock, bounded by another hedge near the ladies' present tee. A small stable accommodated two horses, Tom and Dick, who supplied the power to pull the grass cutters. When the present seventh green was constructed, there was a willow tree on the front left corner which hollowed out in time. (Peggy Reece remembers sheltering right inside it as the waters rose around her! [She escaped – author.])

The men's tee for the next hole was on the flat land on the left of it on the far side of the Trym. The ladies' tee was near the old stone bridge. It was necessary to carry the paddock hedge with the drive to reach the fairway, and this was called the Valley hole.

Our ninth and their 15th followed the same course up the hill from a spot where the ladies' tee is now, and at the top of the ridge, across which people still stroll with dogs as one waits to drive, there ran a hedge out of the trees and across to Sandy Lane. The green was not far the other side – "A bit of a punchbowl on a patch of flat ground," said George.

The player then walked to the ladies' tee of our sixth to play his 16th hole, and there he had to drive over a stone wall, a high one with steps each side. It stretched right across the course to the back of our tenth tee. The only other hazards on this hole were grass bunkers, and it was a bogey five. And so on to the fifth tee under the tree for the 17th, exactly the same as now but shorter. Generally the second shot had to be played short of the wall. The green was just over the other side, and this was flat, with nothing to stop a ball.

Finally, and hopefully not too confusedly, walk up to our tenth tee for the last hole. Lift your eyes up the hill and the first thing you see is the hedge running across the top. Over it you go, and the green is a very small one, not linked to the second. This hole was called The Farm because of the farm mentioned at the first.

Henbury was a tight, hemmed-in course but that was long ago. Things are vastly different now.

# Tales of the Trym

The valley of the Trym was a natural playground for the village boys and girls a hundred years ago, just as Coombe Hill was an attraction for family outings and picnics.

Today, at the age of 80, sprightly Miss Agnes Skyrme, of Westbury, vividly recalls happy times as a child playing in the fields that became the golf course. Her late brother, Arthur, who became one of the best regarded members of the club, shared in the fun with many others, including George Prescott, who later became members.

"Sometimes families would go up to Coombe Hill for a walk or a picnic and would find themselves having to dodge golf balls," says Miss Skyrme. "A favourite place was the fresh water spring at the bottom of the hill opposite the Trym green. It's ruined now, but it was always reckoned that the water had wonderful properties."

It is incredible now to learn that the Trym was navigable by small trading boats more than a thousand years ago. Some cataclysmic tremor that created the Goodwin Sands caused a counter reaction here that effectively reduced the Trym to a winding countryside stream.

Progress has changed its considerable charms for the worse. In Prescott's youth and indeed for long after World War Two it remained a pleasant stretch of clear water in which minnows and sticklebacks abounded. The author well remembers excursions apart from golf at the insistence of a small son armed with net and jamjar as late as the 1950s. Prescott recalls swimming in flood waters!

Before the stream was channelled and containing walls constructed the flooding could be frightening, with water eight to nine feet deep. We still have evidence of this force today when the eighth fairway goes under.

"One day when the water was going down like nobody's business," George recalls, "I saw a boy drown there. He slipped on the bank, and although there were four or five of us, we could not get to him until he had been swept as far downstream as the new bridge. We carried him to Cherry Orchard House, and sent for the doctor. Dr Arnold had to come on his bicycle. The ambulance was sent for, but the lad was dead . . .''

Tales of the Trym are legion. From a golfing point of view the short hole played over the water is outstanding. It can be a frightening hole from the back tee in a medal round, depending on the wind, and one of the priorities of organisation in the running of any major club or county event is to have a rota of intrepid club volunteers as spotters stationed behind the green.

"I have never seen so many terrible shots," said Reg Gerrish, former club captain, after a stint as a spotter in 1965 when John Parker won the City and County championship. "I was in the water most of the time!"

He got some compensation when he saw Ian Fraser of Long Ashton, hole his tee shot. The ball landed a foot past the flagstick and skidded back into the hole. On his second visit in the afternoon Fraser took five.

One lovely afternoon, elderly Mrs King, a dignified, slightly imperious lady, was playing a medal with another, who shall be nameless. The latter put her tee shot in the water. The banks of the stream had not been built up in those days, and she climbed down to retrieve the ball from ankle-deep water. Having done so, she began to climb out, lost a handhold, slipped and sat down with a thump in the middle of the stream.

Stalking across the old wooden bridge on the left, Gertie King heard the noise and looked down to see her partner gazing up in disbelief and disarray.

"Silly thing!" she snorted, and strode on.

---

*Footnote*: Kitchen crisis. Suggestion: A general change of Tradesmen, particularly Biggs, Milkman, who cannot deliver at a reasonable hour (1915).

"Heavy rain last night (Friday) flooded greens and the course greatly benefited. Therefore, most of a small entry beat bogey, W.H. Cavell winning with five up." (July 14, 1923)

# Branching out

Bill Wyatt was a butcher's assistant who grew up to be manager of Ellin's shop in Westbury village; Joe Grigg was a blacksmith and R. Baker was a shop assistant.

These and many more names are easily identified by George Prescott browsing over a newspaper cutting about a match between Henbury and its artisans in May, 1933.

Bertie Young, soon to be chairman, led the club and lost 4 and 2 to Reg Morse; Tom Collins, a big name in the field of domestic industry and particularly in the matter of ovens, lost 4 and 3 to Bill Dent, who still lives in the village at the age of 85. Tim, of the Pearce family of builders, and Ernie Mogford, head of the well-known ironmongery business, took part.

The artisans won 6½-5½, but the club's tail wagged well. Dentist C.G. Plumley, club captain after World War Two, beat Arthur Skyrme, A.E. Metcalfe, manager of the Whitby fashion shops, beat Bill Woodherd; George Meadows, another dentist, beat Wyatt, and S.C. Newton, later to be treasurer and captain, was too much for Charlie Gold and won 6 and 5.

Enthusiasm was the reason for such strong artisan activity in the club. The villagers wanted a share of the golf on Coombe Hill after the Great War, but they were generally chivvied off the course. Various approaches were made to the club about the possibility of forming an artisans and tradesmen's section, but they could not get an ear and were fobbed off again and again. It was not until 1924 that something happened.

Ernest Mogford, a well-known and respected personality who ran the ironmongery business established by his father in Westbury, rounded up as much support for the artisan cause as he could find, and forty of them went along to a meeting in Westbury Post Office on the evening of March 29th.

Mogford, a jaunty, bearded, bespectacled and extremely colourful man, was their secretary. Among many interests was his work as historian in the village, but he was a considerable sportsman and good cricketer. He played golf, but little is known of his prowess in that direction. Nevertheless, he did a great deal of groundwork for the artisans.

Postmaster Fred Bluett presided at this fateful meeting in his office, and club professional Jack Branch went along as a guest speaker. "His attendance was much appreciated, and he gave some interesting and very instructive advice on the rules and etiquette of golf," said Mogford.

Before the evening went much further an artisans' section was formed, and Branch found himself on the committee. The Artisans' Club was sanctioned at the 1924 annual meeting. Rules were strict regarding membership control and hours of play.

"On Sundays," says Prescott, "we had to play 12 holes before 8.30 a.m., and had to get a move on to clear the Punchbowl (our 18th) before then. We certainly didn't waste any time! I can see the lights on Harold Butt's bicycle even now as he used to come riding down to Fisher's place in College Road. He left the bike there, and we cut across the fields to start at the 15th (our ninth). We fairly scooted round!"

Arthur Fisher was a shoe repairer, and a popular, whimsical character who played light-heartedly and enjoyed his golf on the hill for many years after the last war.

The Artisans passed a resolution "desiring to express their keen appreciation and thanks to the committee and members of the Henbury Golf Club for their friendly and neighbourly action in allowing the formation of the Artisans' Club, also for the generous conditions granted, and venture to hope the concession will become permanent."

It took years and years for that to happen. At every annual meeting until 1975 the following appeared on the report: "Artisans' Club. The Committee have sanctioned its continuance for another year on existing terms."

\*   \*   \*

The chauffeur-driven limousine was a familiar sight as it glided through Westbury taking Mr A.R.L. Lobbett to the city.

*Left*, Ernest Mogford. *Above*, Phyllis Lobbett.

53

He sat bolt upright in the back, looking neither right nor left, hands folded on top of a walking stick between his knees. He wore a bowler hat, and presented a somewhat grim, forbidding figure. "I can see him now," says Miss Skyrme. "He always looked lugubrious!" – Lobbett was a landowner, but what had founded his fortune is not known. He lived in an imposing mansion called Henbury Hill – not to be confused with Henbury Hill House – on the site of Westover Close where the magnificent cedar stands today. There was a lodge at the corner of Henbury Hill and Northover Road. Lobbett owned the land from there down to Falcondale Road and back as far as Westbury cricket ground. In modern parlance, he was loaded.

In addition to this he owned a field, or paddock, at the entrance to the golf course, which was opposite the Northover corner in those days (and for many years after), and another field and the woods dropping down from there to the lower course.

The garden of Henbury Hill stretched to the bottom of the hill to the great teak gates that stand now as the entrance to a house called Corners. Those gates cost £300, and were hung with great ceremony.

Lobbett does not seem to have played much golf, but his wife did, and his daughter, Phyllis, became famous as an England international. Nevertheless, he did a great deal for Henbury, serving on committee and helping financially, and his wife became ladies' captain in the 1920s.

On one occasion just after the Great War, when a new lease was being negotiated with Harford, the question of £150 expenditure for a field was considered.

"I'll give you £100 of it," Mr Lobbett told the committee, "but you'll have to make me a life member. And my wife," he added.

It was a great deal of money in those days, and the committee jumped at the offer and its condition. In fact life membership was bestowed on Mr and Mrs Lobbett and Phyllis.

Phyllis was the first of Henbury's Big Three who put the club into prominence, the others much later being Peggy Reece and Malcolm Lewis. Apart from occasional references to Mrs A.R. Lobbett and Miss P. in some of the ladies' records before the Great War, there was nothing to indicate that the girl was other than an ordinary club player.

However, the *Western Daily Press* of March 25th, 1914, described her as "a young lady who has not been playing much more than two years, who possesses a good style and should go far".

From that time until 1921 when she reached the Somerset county final and was beaten by Dolly Fowler, nothing is known of Phyllis Lobbett, but she had obviously done enough to be selected for England in 1922. She played in the Home Internationals again in 1924-27-29-30.

She achieved foursomes fame in partnership with Miss Fowler who again had the better of her in the Somerset county finals of 1923-4-5, and together they won the London Ladies Foursomes in 1924-29-30 and Eve's Northern Foursomes in 1929. Phyllis competed regularly on the continent, and in 1928 won the Dutch Ladies championship at Zandvoort.

From 1930 nothing more was heard of her, and it is a story without ending as far as the author is concerned. Miss Wanda Morgan wrote recently to say: "All I can tell you myself is that she was tall, rather quiet, well built, one could say. I remember her as rather awe-inspiring, but I was very young myself then!"

A group of artisans in mid 1920s, including George Morse, Tom Evans, George Lavis, Arthur Fisher and E. Baker.

---

*Footnote*: CAPERN'S No. 1 is the golf ball for you, 2s. each, and in three weights, to suit all golfers – Capern's Golf Ball Co., Portland Square, Bristol.

# Sandy Young

For more than thirty years Sandy Young was a leading personality as a player and administrator in Gloucestershire and Somerset golf. He was a member of Henbury for most of that time, but subsequently bought Berrow Manor opposite the old Church Hole at Burnham and Berrow.

His daughter, Ruth Mary, recalls "spending hours on the putting green at Henbury, but, alas, it did not make me any good at putting! I remember that during the war my father used to cycle occasionally from Stoke Bishop for a round at Henbury."

Those who remember C.H. Young automatically associate him with Somerset golf, and rightly so for he played for the county for many years. What is not appreciated is that he first played for Gloucestershire in 1926 and played top against Somerset.

The following year he began a long career with Somerset by playing top for them against Gloucestershire. He played everywhere in those days and a great deal at Burnham, but his base was Henbury.

He was club captain in 1930, and became a director and chairman of Henbury Properties until his retirement in 1951. He was a chartered accountant and company director with offices in Exchange Chambers, Corn Street, in which he would frequently preside over golf club business meetings.

It was written of Sandy Young that "No one does more for the progress of the game in this area. He has been hon treasurer of the Gloucestershire and Somerset Alliance since its inception, and honorary secretary of the South Western Counties Association since its formation. He's a great organiser."

Sandy was a fine card-and-pencil player who regularly produced scores in the sixties at Henbury, but county success was to elude him. He was runner-up to Stanley Dickinson in the 1925 Somerset championship, and runner-up to J.A.

Pierson in the 1928 West of England championship, both events being played at Burnham.

In a Henbury club match on July 13, 1929, Young went round in 66 with eight fours, eight threes and par fives at the 13th and 14th (our fifth and sixth). It was the best ever done by an amateur over the course played with that lay-out, but it could not count as a record.

In September, 1936, he won the Arthur Cup with six up on bogey after another round of 66, and a week later equalled his own record of 64 (which is nowhere recorded) to win the Ashmead Cup with 63 nett. He kept on doing that sort of thing. His great strength was iron play.

The author knew Sandy Young in his later Burnham days, and recalls a late September evening as he practised on his own on the eve of the West of England championship.

"I was hitting shots along the old dogleg 13th, which is now a housing estate, and was suddenly aware of a figure standing on the top of the bank on the right of the fairway. It was Sandy, using a hickory two-iron as a walking stick, on his way home from the clubhouse.

"We talked for some minutes, assessing the field for the coming event, and he wanted all the Henbury news. Then, with a wave, he went his way into the gathering dusk. I never saw him again."

\* \* \*

It was a wet, dismal day in June, 1927, but it was a festive occasion when a group of Henbury members "spent a happy day at Nailsea, everyone enjoying golf against Nailsea – and a football match".

Henbury players were part of a Bristol team led by W. 'Fatty' Wedlock, the famous footballer who had played "remarkably good golf".

"They fielded twelve men, and nobody noticed! Jack Branch was in goal and before many minutes had elapsed the ball trickled slowly between his legs. He thought this was a huge joke . . ." The day ended with skittles at the Royal Oak.

* * *

Sam Meaker, one of Henbury's leading artisans, won the Filton open competition for the Lord Mayor's Christmas Dinner Fund for Children. He received five shots and finished one up, the only player in a large field to beat bogey. He beat Harry Pruett, Fred Jewell, Charlie Pixton and cricketer Charlie Parker.

Meaker won "a nice fireside chair" presented by G.H.J. Osborne, one of Filton's oldest members. He immediately put it up for raffle and it fetched £4.3.0.

On an earlier Christmas occasion at Henbury a sweep for the same charity resulted in a box at the Hippodrome for R.E. Armstrong.

* * *

After 21 years as hon secretary to the Gloucestershire Union, George Talbot Plum retired in February, 1927. He was commended at the annual meeting at the Wellington Hotel, Gloucester, for "yeoman service to the union," and was made president-elect. Talbot Plum who, according to Miss Skyrme, was always a leading light in Westbury affairs, was Henbury captain in 1929.

* * *

Major Archdale, a dominant figure of the club's early days, collapsed and died in his office at Burnham and Berrow only a few hours after the West of England amateur final involving Sandy Young and Pierson in 1928.

"When he was stationed at Horfield Barracks he was a member of Henbury," wrote Bunker. "He was a scratch player in his youth. In the 1890s he played cricket for his regiment and E.M. Grace's team at Thornbury with more than ordinary ability. He played polo during army life in India.

"Archdale, spectacles on the end of his nose and with his beloved pipe, was a greatly respected figure as secretary of

C.H. 'Sandy' Young.

Burnham and recognised by the club as an authority on greenkeeping and course construction. He was responsible for many improvements at Burnham and Berrow."

* * *

William Windus was elected club captain and president in 1910 following the death of Arthur Baker. He became one of the oldest members, and a regular player who was "a genial and generous man".

Only a few days before his death in 1928 at the age of 75 Bill Windus followed with vim and vigour the first 18 holes of a club match. At times George Prescott caddied for him, and recalls a regular fourball with a Mr Veale partnering Windus against George Riseley, who for 50 years was organist at the Colston Hall, and Pip Marshall, a master at St John's School at the top of Blackboy Hill. Riseley was a lively 82 at the time.

* * *

Denys Cavell is remembered as a 'young' senior of the club in 1946, and as a very capable player.

Frank Preston, club secretary in the early 1920s, had a high opinion of him. He forecast a county place for Cavell who "has a good physique, youth and the right kind of temperament".

On a day when nett 95 won at Burnham, with gusts up to 100 mph, thirty people braved it at Henbury. It is on record that "there was not only a hurricane but the light was very trying. And Cavell, receiving only two shots, finished one down."

"Cavell is the sort of person who might be expected to do well in adverse conditions," wrote Preston. "He hits a long ball with low trajectory, and has the invaluable knack of maintaining body balance. During the past three or four years he has accomplished many fine performances. At one Henbury meeting he swept the board."

Cavell won the Knock-out Cup in 1931 and '33, and for a third time after fourteen years and a world war in 1947.

*  *  *

Major M. Wilkins retired in 1936 after eleven years as Henbury secretary – a fact that put paid to Jack Estill's hope that he had created a record in that office with nine-and-a-half years when he retired last November.

Bunker had this to say: "During this period the Major, as he was affectionately known to all the members, has been not only a highly efficient official but a most popular one, and his retirement is regretted by one and all, including the members of the Press to whom he was always most courteous and of the greatest assistance.

"The Major has been made an honorary member. He is not leaving Bristol, and will be seen about the course."

The new secretary was R.L. Brown from Mannings Heath, Sussex, and it was his first such post. He played off eight.

*  *  *

E. Pearce Dyment won the 1924 July medal by five strokes with 82-14-68.

"This was a popular win," said the *Evening News*, "and well merited the honour conferred upon him by the Handicap committee of a reduction in handicap."

---

*Footnote*: The stewardess considered she was entitled to a glass of ale with each of two meals . . . Agreed (September 10, 1915).

# Money Matters

In 1931 the club grasped the opportunity to buy the freehold of the course from the Blaise estate for £8,000.

As land could not be held in the name of a club, it was immediately necessary to put it in the names of individuals or corporation. This prompted the decision to form a limited company to hold the land on behalf of the club. Money had to be raised for the purchase price, and so Henbury Properties Ltd came into being to do it by way of mortgage and the issue of debentures to members. The company's share capital consisted of 100 £1 Ordinary shares, of which only five were issued. These were held in the names of four directors and one held jointly by the secretary and treasurer of the club. There is no beneficial interest to shareholders who are purely nominees of the club.

In effect, the club owns the company and all its assets, mainly the land and the clubhouse.

Major Sampson Way, Ernest Ashmead, Alfred Evans and Raymond J. Watts, solicitor, held the first company meeting at the offices of Hudson Smith Briggs and Co at Exchange Chambers on Friday, August 14th.

The first hint of what was to happen some twenty years later is contained in a minute of a 1934 meeting:

"The board (of Henbury Properties) considered fully a letter from the City Engineer asking if the company would have the lower holes of the course set down as an open space in the Town Planning scheme . . .

It was carried unanimously that no alteration should be made in the present arrangement, which is that the lower part of the course is reserved for building."

In 1956 Henbury had two great assets – astute directors, and an enormous hole in the ground, the quarry, no less.

The 1954 Town and Country Planning Act allowed under certain conditions claims for £21,530 in the case of Henbury, being the difference between the unrestricted and restricted value of the land. The eighty odd acres were shown as an open private space, and Mr Belmont Strange, acting for the club, said the chances were 99 in a hundred that any building proposition would be turned down flat. In a nutshell Henbury offered to build houses on the course, knowing very well that this would not happen, and was refused permission. Bristol's Labour-controlled Planning committee decided that the course, crossed by three public footpaths, was more valuable as an open space.

So the golf club was compensated for loss of development rights with a cheque for £22,514. As Belmont Strange told the directors: "We are not pulling a fast one, but only doing what we are allowed to by law." The money came from a £300 million Government fund.

A political storm broke out. Alderman Wally Hennessy, Planning committee chairman, told the newspapers: "I regard their claim as legalised robbery – and there's nothing we can do about it. The club knew very well that no committee would agree to houses going up on this beautiful land." He went on: "When the compensation fund was set up by the Labour Government after the war it was not intended that money should be given away in this manner."

In answer to this club secretary Charles Griffey told the Press: "We only exercised our rights, as individuals and organisations have been doing all over the country."

"What will the club do with the money?" the *Evening Post* asked him. Griffey said an extraordinary general meeting will discuss this. "We shall probably decide to build ourselves a nice new clubhouse in place of the old wooden one which is practically falling down. The only other thing the club is likely to spend money on is course improvements that it has not been able to carry out in the past owing to financial stringency."

In 1958 tenders were invited for the building of a new clubhouse, and Benson Brothers came up with £19,886. Henbury had £19,732 and an arranged mortgage of £4,000, making £23,732. The signal was clear: Go ahead.

A year later, on June 24th, 1959, Henbury possessed the best clubhouse in the west country, a sentiment expressed by hundreds of members. It was designed by architect John Day, a member of the club at that time, and there was never anything but praise. The official opening ceremony was performed by H.S. Young the president who had been a member for more than thirty years, and a stone commemorates the occasion and his name on the front wall of the clubhouse at the side of the main entrance.

It was a proud moment for Bertie Young, and for Bernard O'Brien and Herbert Brook who had had so much to do with the original dream and steering the project through the teething stages to this happy climax.

Charles Griffey.

---

*Footnote*: "Every effort has been made to get rid of the mice but the Rodent Control Officer of the Corporation now admits that it is apparently beyond his powers. A cat will therefore have to be obtained, and it is hoped he/she will succeed where man has failed." (1970 minute)

# The Big Deal

Now for the continuing saga of the hole in the ground.

Ever since 1954 the club had eyed the Cherry Orchard to the west of the southern slopes of the lower part of the course. This was on the other side of the hedge running across our third fairway at the ridge. We needed more length, and that would be ideal.

C.H. Hewitt, the man who leased the quarry and paid us some royalties on the stone he removed, was always agitating for more ground. He badgered club management incessantly for permission to quarry still further.

So a deal was struck with Mr Hewitt. If he bought Cherry Orchard in his name and transferred it to Henbury Properties he would have a ten-year lease of extension of the quarry westwards for 45 yards, plus a five-yards footpath . . .

Hewitt bought the land for £600. It was stipulated that he was to clear away the boundary hedge, extend the fairway, make the present third green and the new fourth.

The work on the course was poorly done, mistakes with drains, poor soil, a quarryman's outlook rather than a greenkeeper's and a certain amount of dragging of feet, made for aggravation all round. It was not until late 1957 that the new holes were opened, but they made all the difference. New back tees were made at five holes, and the overall length of the course increased by 300 yards to just under 6,000.

The value of the hole in the ground became apparent in 1966 when, after much procrastination and changing of plans, together with what seems to have been a staggering amount of ineptitude, Hewitt suggested filling in the quarry.

A year later Henbury invited tenders, and with land for tipping at a premium even the City Council joined the queue. Eventually the club accepted from Wring and Co a figure of £2,000 a year for a minimum of five years for filling in the quarry. It was a gargantuan task causing considerable upheaval, more haggling and argument with contractors, and it went on for seven years. The final topping up in 1973 coincided with development of the Trym area which culminated in the laying of culverts to prevent flooding.

Finally everything was in order. It had taken a long time, and the exercise of great patience. The course gained some two hundred yards to its present length and a standard scratch 70 instead of 69. The 14th was extended to its present 530, and the 15th stretched from 380 to 430. The 14th was named after the late chairman, Bernard Windebank, and his family planted a copse of trees there to his memory.

The Henbury course had reached its limits on the ground. All that remained was to make the very best use of it.

The quarry. Over the top of that face was the 14th green.

*Footnote*: "There being complaints of the stewardess as to her manners and conduct to members (i.e. being abrupt and not obliging) it was agreed that a change was desirable." (1931)

# Major Roles

Life was never dull in the presence of Gwynne Vevers who steered the fortunes of the club for 16 years, up to World War Two and immediately afterwards. He was a director of Henbury Properties in the beginning with Ernest Ashmead, Sampson Way, Becket Hurst, C.H. Young and H.G. Treasure.

Vevers was the son of a Hereford farmer and born to hunting, shooting and fishing. Golf was one of his sporting loves, but he was an accomplished soccer player and one time chairman of Bristol City F.C. He retired as club chairman in 1947, and died in 1953 after a long illness. He is remembered by the Gwynne Vevers Foursomes trophy, one of the most popular events on the club's playing calendar.

Major roles were played in the post-war years by Herbert Young, Herbert Brook, Bernard O'Brien; Freddie Bate and Bernard Windebank, insurance and bank managers; George Dewfall, Maurice Herbert, C.G. Plumley, Jack Dutton and Arthur Staniland.

The affable Frank Davis took over from the unflappable David Williams as secretary in 1948. Williams had been in office before the war and he kept the club operating all the time. He died in 1954 at the age of 77. For eight years Davis held office. He had retired in 1954 and handed over to Bill Simmonds but the latter's health broke down, and Davis was recalled, frustrated once again in his expressed desire to "retire and play golf in peace".

Ralph Wyatt came on the scene to replace Davis. He lived at Almondsbury and had given up the secretaryship of Bristol & Clifton "because the journey was a bit too much". Wyatt was a retired bank manager who had started his golf at Romford during the Great War. For a time he lived at Warminster and played at West Wilts. It was a short relationship with Henbury. Wyatt died in 1957.

Maurice Herbert was club captain in 1955. He was born in Ireland, educated in Bath and in his youth a considerable soccer player and cricketer. He played for Knowle C.C. for many years, and also represented Gloucestershire in small bore rifle shooting. He had played golf for 16 years and had a handicap of six when he became captain. For five years he was match secretary, three years chairman of greens and also sat on the county committee.

In his captaincy Maurice won the Challenge Cup with 68-6-62, but only by a shot from George Dewfall.

Dewfall, the gentle giant, stood six feet four, but "Jack Dutton beat me by an inch!" He, too, was a familiar figure in local cricket, a fast bowler for Schoolmasters C.C. who twice played for Gloucestershire, and he played forward for Old Cothamians at rugby. In his long years of membership George was on the committee for three and was match secretary for two.

He had many playing successes. He was elected chairman in 1967 when the *Evening Post* said: "Henbury are sitting right on top of the west country golf world.

"They have a new subscription record of £6,680, green fees of over £1,000, a year's trading profit of £1,300, and a total membership of 580, with a long waiting list.

"An inscribed gold watch and a silver tankard were presented to the retiring chairman, Herbert Brook, who was elevated to the presidency, and Freddie Bate, the retiring captain."

\*   \*   \*

Of all the cricketers who played at Henbury the most famous were the Graveney brothers, Tom and Ken, but long ago there was a W.S.A. Brown who played as an amateur on an occasional basis around the turn of the century.

The writer is indebted to Vic Parkes for unearthing the following information about him: "Brown was a 'lower order' batsman but good enough to knock up 89 against Sussex in 1900 at Brighton (Ranjitsinhji was playing for the opposition!).

"The same year saw him open the Gloucestershire innings with 66 against the West Indians at Bristol."

W.S.A. Brown and his wife were Henbury members, but any golfing prowess on their part was never recorded.

Tom Graveney was the better of the brothers in the early 1950s but Ken went on to greater things later, winning the county championship in 1968. He captained the team, and was subsequently elected county president.

Tom played down to one handicap, and he won many club trophies, including the Knock-out Cup and Scratch Cup each three times.

The secret of Tom's game was his ability to "miss 'em straight". His cricketer's left forearm crunched through the impact zone and he hit long, straight shots with ease. His reputation for big hitting was fully justified. One evening, in response to a challenge, he stood on the tee of the old Drop Hole at the far side of our 18th green and proceeded to pound balls on to the Trym green!

*Far left*, Ken Graveney deputised for brother Tom on April 10th, 1958, for the presentation of the Graveney Cup. This group was taken before the result was known. Picture includes a young David Windebank, third from right, next to club captain Stanley Hardiman. *Left*, George Dewfall.

*Footnote*: Numerous complaints made about people cutting in on the course. Uproar over people cleaning clubs in the washbasins (1912). Canon Charles Parry Way back at the club as a five-day member (1927.

# The Legend

Jack Harrison strode on to the Henbury scene in 1955 and built a legend in his own time. He was no stranger to members, having been for years the kingpin of Knowle and a leading figure in the county. He won trophies galore, but rather like his Henbury predecessor Sandy Young could not win titles, other than one in the Far East which earned him the label of Chinese champion. He played for Wales in the Home Internationals of 1937 and '50.

He had been captain of Knowle, and reached the final of the West of England championship against Jack Payne at Burnham in 1951. He lost 3 and 1, but he was unwell. At the end of the game he collapsed and found himself in hospital with a cracked up heart.

Jack was on the golfing sidelines for some three years and living in Cardiff, but brought his family back to live in Westbury. It was imperative that he should join Henbury, and after that happened neither party regretted it.

In the years that followed Jack invigorated club and county. He was the best player, subject at times to signs and portents, extrovert but extremely practical. He got things done.

The City and County of Bristol championship was his project, and he was determined it should be the best of all. In his time he won the Ashton Vase, and in 1963 he took Henbury's Scratch Cup for the third time in a row by eleven shots. The following year he was president of Gloucestershire, and presented his club with the Coombe Hill Cup for the player having the best four consecutive medal rounds.

Guy Randel was a colourful, loquacious character, brisk with ruddy complexion, brushy moustache, plus fours, and cap at a rakish angle. He was a good golfer, and he possessed a further attribute in his ability to talk the hind leg off a donkey.

It is perhaps unfair that he should be remembered for this in conjunction with his outstanding victory over W.S. Wise in the final of the county championship at Stinchcombe Hill. Randel was astute enough to realise from experience that Wise had a reputation for vocal diversion during golf.

There was never more than two holes between the two men, with Wise thirty yards ahead off the tee and Randel inside him on the greens. Randel won by one hole, but Bill Wise had never before met anyone who could out-talk him on a golf course.

Earlier in 1954 Randel was beaten 2 and 1 by Arthur Skyrme in the final of the Knock-out Cup.

Skyrme was a fine all-round sportsman who completed the rare double that year of winning the Scratch Cup as well, three strokes ahead of Ken Graveney and Nick Carter. He was one of the original artisans, an engineer and, of course, a contemporary of George Prescott. He was one of the most popular of club members.

In his early days Arthur played football for Gloucestershire, and had a considerable reputation as a fast right arm bowler for Westbury C.C. All his days – and nights – he was a formidable snooker player.

As far as Arthur was concerned the club's annual meeting in April, 1973, seemed like any other he had attended. And so it was, until the moment retiring chairman Bernard Windebank announced that Arthur had been made an honorary member. Applause was unanimous, the surprise complete.

Charles Griffey decided to retire from the secretaryship in 1966 and move with his wife to Sidmouth where he had always wanted to live. His birthplace was Bideford, and he learned his golf at Westward Ho! which explains why he held a single figure handicap for more than fifty years. He was a retired schoolmaster, working in Bristol between the wars. He was club captain in 1954 and secretary for ten years, holding office through some of the thinnest years and on into the thickest.

Charles Moffatt (and his *Times* crossword) followed Griffey but stood down after two years, succeeded by Bill Pluck who had returned from Uganda after many years in government service, a period including the secretaryships of several golf clubs.

Bernard Windebank did a great deal for Henbury in several capacities. He was treasurer from 1962–66 after which he became captain. He was a director of the property company in 1961, and club chairman in 1969, handing over this office to Keith Turner in 1973.

Bernard's son David first drew attention to himself in 1959 by going to Shirehampton Park and winning the Tait Cup in the county junior championship with a score of 76.

Five years later he won the club's Scratch Cup by two from Ian Clarke with 148. Shortly afterwards he gave up competitive golf to pursue his career in the jewellery business, and did not return to it until 1971.

It was an outstanding come-back. He played for Gloucestershire in the early part of that season, won the Scratch Cup, and also took the Scratch Knock-out Cup at Long Ashton.

David was the first golfer to captain the county at junior, colt and senior levels. In 1977 he took Gloucestershire through to the English County finals at Saunton, and they finished second to Warwickshire. He is now serving on the English Golf Union Executive and junior golf committees. Some of the game's highest offices are in his stars.

When L.C. Carter took office as captain in 1963 the ladies' captain was Mrs Elsie Stoker. "You are in the fortunate position," he told members at the annual meeting, "of being led by two Elsies!"

L.C. has been Nick to all and sundry for so long that he may possibly have forgotten what his initials stand for. He joined the club when his war years ended, and the quality of his golf was exceptional, particularly because of the unorthodoxy of the method.

Nick's style typified the maxim of "not how, but how many," and there was a spell when he won just about everything in the club. Scores of 70 and 69 were regulation stuff, but he also produced them under pressure, and that made him different.

One memorable occasion was at Stinchcombe Hill when he partnered Maurice Herbert in a Gloucester and Somerset Alliance bogey. They won with nine up! They combined perfectly. Between them they lost eleven holes, yet only one of those losses appeared on the card. They won eleven, and ten of them went down. The following appeared in the *Western Daily Press* of July 26, 1957:

> Then Carter ran into brilliant form. What this experienced golfer lacks in style he more than compensates for in determination and concentration.
>
> . . . with his somewhat peculiar hand action and short swing he can punch a ball so far, and around the

greens he is a dogged finisher.

He has done many good things at Henbury, but he will look back on this display at Stinchcombe with particular pleasure. From the short ninth to the 17th inclusive he went 3 4 2 4 4 3 3 3 4 against the card's 3 4 3 4 5 4 3 4 4, and he completed the round in 70 after taking 38 to the turn.

Nick Carter still plays in the mornings, likes to walk the course with a dog in the afternoons, and listens to his beloved music in the evenings. Few know the place so well, and very few can love it more.

Jack Harrison.

---

*Footnote*: Holes order changes again, making our 11th the first, round ending on our first and second (1928).

# Winning Golf

Bill Branch was 19 when he was nominated for the Ryder Cup in January, 1931.

He had claimed attention by winning the Assistants' championship at Moseley the previous season, but subsequently he failed in the trials and was not selected.

Bill was born at Alsager, Cheshire, in 1911, the year before his father Jack came to Henbury as professional, and he grew up on Coombe Hill as one of the boys with Prescott and company. At 17 he went round the course in 65, everything holed, playing with E.I.M. Davey. The course was played in the following order (these are our present numbers):

Out – 1st, 2nd, 11th, 14th, 15th, 16th, 13th, 12th, 17th, equals 37; In – 18th, Drop, 3rd, 5th, 6th, 7th, 8th, 9th, 10th equals 36. Total 73.

Branch had nine threes and no twos: Out – 4 5 3 4 4 4 3 3 3 – 33; in – 3 3 3 5 3 3 4 4 4 – 32.

Some time later when the top holes were played in today's order but the Drop was still in existence, he went round in 61 (30, 31), the card being marked by J. Evans. This card is reproduced, but there is no year on it.

After his well publicised 65, Bill was appointed assistant to James Horn at Weston-super-Mare. In 1930, the year of his national break-through in the Assistants' championship, Bill partnered Sandy Young to win the Alliance Inter-Club Foursomes for Henbury. He must have left Weston. Young had also won this title with Jack Branch in 1926.

Bill won the Gloucester and Somerset match play title at Burnham, beating the redoubtable home professional A.R. Bradbeer 6 and 5 over 36 holes. In 1932 he won the West of England title and the Midlands Assistants' championship.

Sandy and Bill teamed up again in 1934 and reached the final of the Alliance Foursomes again by beating Knowle (A.W. Esbester and Sid Easterbrook) by 3 and 2 at Long Asthon in the semi-finals.

That same year Bill won the famous Palace Hotel Short Course championship at Torquay with a record aggregate of 195.

The next year he beat Henry Cotton, Alf Padgham, Alf Perry the Open champion and Sid Brews to tie with Flory van Donck for the Belgian Open at Brussels, and won the play off by four strokes. In Perry's Open at Muirfield that summer Branch came ninth with 71, 73, 76 and 74, a stroke behind Cotton and Easterbrook.

Henbury made father and son honorary members in 1937 when Jack celebrated 25 years "as an old and valuable servant with the club". The tribute to Bill, who had already played for England, was in recognition of "his fine performances in national and other events which have done much to maintain Henbury's position in the golfing world". That same day W.J. left to be professional at Leicester.

After many more successes and moves, Bill went to Ganton and dominated Yorkshire professional golf through the 1950s, winning five open titles. He later moved to Fulford, retired from there in 1977 and died in February, 1985.

Jack Branch soldiered on for another twelve years, living in a house he named Sunningdale behind the bus stop in Falcondale Road at the bottom of Henbury Hill. In his later days he rarely left the clubhouse putting green, always making useful pocket money by putting for pennies with an old Mills club. There was a time when he would play 18 holes against all and sundry with that implement alone. The club was saddened by his death in 1949 after 36 years "as faithful friend and professional".

Branch's successor was Jim Blundell, a senior assistant with former Open champion Richard Burton at Coombe Hill, Surrey.

"Welcome to Coombe Hill," the author greeted him.

"You mean goodbye," he said, "I've just come from there."

"No, welcome. This Coombe Hill has been a golf club twenty years longer than the place in Surrey!"

*Far left*, William Branch. *Left*, Alan Mawson, professional for 28 years.

76

# 'Mr Nice Guy'

Clubs slung across his back, Alan Mawson rode into Bristol astride a motor-cycle in 1952, and liked what he saw.

The members also liked what they saw and appointed him professional in succession to Blundell who had gravitated towards the south coast. (Blundell now lives in retirement in Cheshire).

The Mawson relationship was to last 28 years. The contract ended in 1980 but the friendship went on for Mawson was made an honorary member. Ill health really forced Mawson out, and on his retirement he was the oldest serving professional in Bristol.

He came from Bedford with a good teaching reputation and most of the armament required to be a competitor. Shortly afterwards Bedford realised what they had lost, and wanted him back, but Mawson had found his home. He settled, raised a family and soon made an impact on the local professional scene.

In the 1959 Open at Muirfield, won by Gary Player, Mawson shot 69 in the first qualifying round and gained national newspaper headlines. His play was described by Henbury's Stuart Gibson, who went round with him, as "one of the most copybook displays I have ever seen. Mawson can play golf as well as any of the others." If he lapsed from grace under the subsequent pressure, the critics had noted his worth.

His son Peter grew up at Henbury with a club in his hand, and when he was eventually appointed to Filton at the age of 19 he was the youngest full club professional in the country. For years he has been successfully established at Bristol & Clifton.

Bob Newton was a popular successor to Alan. He had been trained for a couple of years by Richard Bradbeer at Burnham and Berrow. He was 24 with ambition and good credentials but somehow life changed for him, and eventually he withdrew from the professional game.

He was followed in 1986 by Peter Stow, a disciple of the famous John Jacobs, but after four years here the chance of returning to his roots in Surrey came up with a vacancy at Hankley Common. It was impossible for him to ignore this, and when he went he took Henbury's Brendan Wynne as assistant.

Nick Riley is now settling in as the new professional, and he should gain much encouragement from the many and varied activities of centenary year. We wish him well.

Alun Williams, with the league trophy, and his Henbury team (1969).

---

*Footnote*: The serious question of the players' neglect in replacing divots led to a circular to all members and a request to report offenders to the secretary (1921).

# Leading Ladies

Mothers and daughters made up much of the early membership of the club. Some of the ladies' teams included as many as four players of the same name, and while it does not follow that they were all one family it seems likely.

In the first years Agnes Fry was a leading figure and consistent match winner off eight handicap. A Mr A.M. Fry of Cambridge Park was an original member in 1891, but there was then no mention of a Miss Fry. Yet in 1896 Agnes was not only ladies' secretary but a member of the general committee. And when she played top for Henbury the second in the team was Miss A.P. Fry who played off four!

In 1900 Agnes Fry and Frances Robinson played for Gloucestershire against Middlesex at Ranelagh. Miss Fry won and Miss Robinson halved, but the county lost 4 to 5.

In the next decade Mrs Windsor Aubrey got down to scratch and played for the county. Family names were to the fore . . . May and Nora Harsant, the Aldridge sisters, names unknown, Mrs Langley and her daughter, Miss G.V. Guise and Miss E.F. Guise, Mrs Bertram Matthews and Miss K. Matthews, two Sampson Ways and numerous Bakers including Miss G. Watkins Baker, Agnes and Miss M.

Mrs Matthews, Mrs Langley and Miss G. Guise played to single figures at this time. One of the first to win a significant county event was Miss D.S. Aldridge who took the Coronation Medals at Henbury with 104-21-83.

Miss M. Wreford Brown caused a stir during the Easter meeting of 1910 by returning 58 nett, going round in 82 with a 24 handicap. An entry in the competition book reads: "There would appear to be some grounds for revising this lady's handicap!"

Ladies' golf had good coverage in the Bristol newspapers, and a *Western Daily Press* report of the 1913 spring meeting was typical:

Though the weather kept fine, competitors had great difficulty in keeping their scores down owing to the exceptionally strong wind which prevailed on both days, and for another reason, owing to circumstances over which those responsible had no control, the grass on the lower side was long in places, so that on occasions the players found that after a good drive the lie was not of the best, and there was some difficulty in getting their second shots away. The greens, however, were in splendid order, and their condition was most favourably commented on.

As usual at Henbury the competitors were divided into two sections, and even taking into consideration that the second division ladies had an advantage in playing two rounds of the ladies' course, they certainly did better, especially the leaders, than those in the first division.

Wreford Brown, then off 18 (the 1910 hint of revision having worked to some degree), won in division one with 101-18-83, and Miss M.M. Morgan in the second division scored 90-21-69. Mrs Aubrey, off three, took 107 . . .

Just before the outbreak of war in 1914 the Gloucestershire county championship was staged at Henbury "in beautiful weather, and was supported by players from all parts of the county. There were 46 entries – an increase of about ten on last year's numbers." Miss Bryan of Minchinhampton won with 174 (82, 92), and Henbury came second to Minchinhampton in the team championship.

When war came Vincent Barnard was club president and Harry Andrews was still secretary. Mrs Barnard was lady captain and continued in office throughout the war and on until 1921. There were 91 lady members in 1914.

Up to that time the lady secretaries had been Miss G.V. Guise, of Coombe House, Westbury, Miss F.G. Robinson, of Sneyd Park, for five years, Miss Alice Rose, of Royal York Crescent, who joined in 1897, Miss E. Hemingway, of Stoke Bishop, who also became county secretary until 1923, and Miss Tryon, of Hallen Lodge, who was lady captain in 1912. As well as Miss Rose, there were Mr H.M. Rose and the Rev Rose.

Three players named Collins played in the first team in the 1920s. Mrs W.R. Collins was captain in 1925, and in her team was Miss D. Collins who was said to have "a lengthy list of golfing successes." A Miss E. Collins appeared at almost the same time, and on occasion all three were in the team together. It would be remarkable if they were unrelated.

One dismal day the ladies had to visit Bath and play at Sham Castle in dense fog. Local instinct rather than knowledge was the only asset that day, and they had none of it. Henbury lost every match, which prompted a written account in the record book: "Bath ladies were merciless. Was it true," the report went on, "or the fanciful carrying of a voice in the mist? – 'Of course they beat us. They were twice our age!'"

An impassioned plea to members to do all in their power to help the captain and hon secretary, and generally strive for friendliness together, was made by a Miss Taylor at the 1926 general meeting. There is no hint why such an exhortation was thought necessary.

It is the writer's fervent hope that future club records will be guarded for posterity's sake because some eight months of frustrating research has gone into making up for the present generation's lost books. This sentiment is expressed as reaction to a minute written after a ladies' meeting in 1930: "The secretary stated that she had a large box of papers and old records, spreading over a number of years, and handed on by her predecessors, and she was instructed to go through them and destroy anything which was valueless."

What one would give sixty years later for the "valueless" contents of that box . . .

---

*Footnote*: May 28th, 1926. One dozen spoons were purchased from Messrs Kemps', Union Street, the club paying for them. – Edith E. Pettit, Hon. Sec.

# The Bait . . .

When Major Sampson Way succeeded Ernest Ashmead as chairman in 1926 he delighted the ladies by offering a salmon as a prize for one of their competitions. It became quite a custom and a happy outcome of the gallant major's angling propensities.

There was Judge Paterson, too, who sometimes gave a box of balls as a prize.

The ladies' section flourished, and there seemed to be almost too many trophies to be played for. It was difficult to include them all in the calendar. The county championship returned to the club in 1933 for the first time since 1914 and was won for the seventh time by Miss Vivien Bramwell, of Long Ashton, who beat Mrs Prettejohn (Lilley Brook) 4 and 2. Mrs Edith E. Harris was captain in succession to Mrs Carruthers, but for some obscure reason the championship did not get a mention in the records.

Club life seems to have gone smoothly until the second outbreak of war in 1939. Kay Collier, whose husband John was one of the characters of the men's club, had reached the final of the county championship in 1934 and been beaten by Miss Bramwell. She got her revenge when Henbury staged the event a third time in 1939, beating Miss Bramwell 2 and 1 over 36 holes. The *Bristol Evening Post* golf writer was quite carried away:

"Two down after the first round, two down after 27 holes, then she appeared to be imbued with the spirit of her brother, Captain Angell James, V.C., for she fought back so gallantly as to win the 29th and square at the 31st. She won the 33rd to take the lead, and the next to win the title. A very fine fight."

Kay held the title until the resumption of play in 1947. She later became county president.

The author remembers both of them, but will never forget John, a stockily built, rosy-cheeked man who looked more countryman than solicitor, standing beneath a tree in the club car park during a thunderstorm . . . His playing companions had quit the course but he refused to go in. "If the Old Boy up there" – jerking a thumb skywards – "wants to write me off with lightning just becos I'm wearing metal studs in m' shoes, it's too bad," he hooted.

He refused to budge, and when the storm abated the other three came into the sunshine, refreshed by several cups of tea, to resume the fourball.

Competitors outside the old clubhouse at the ladies open meeting on June 4th, 1957.

*Footnote*: Public conveyance from Henbury to Westbury and Bristol was "a substantial carriage or wagon" licensed by John Porch and Thomas Coleman. Carried 12 passengers inside protected from the weather by a canopy. Three outside. Twice a day on certain days, changing horses at the Porter Stores, now Blaise Inn (1899).

# What to do in War

A ladies' meeting was held on September 4th, 1939, with the captain, Mrs F.J. Todd, in the chair, those present being Mesdames Gardner, Maggs and Tripp. An apology was received from Mrs Brown.

In view of the war with Germany it was unanimously decided as follows:

1, To cancel the Open meeting, all matches, fixtures and annual competitions;

2, To recall all cups, trophies, these to be held by the club until the end of hostilities;  .

3, To continue the monthly medal and bogey competitions through 1940;

4, All records and finance to be handed over to the club at the end of the financial year if necessary;

5, 1939 captain, secretary and committee to hold office for the duration of war or until the next ladies' general meeting.

Three more meetings took place until May, 1940, but nothing more went on record until February 20th, 1943, when David Williams, then club secretary, presided over a ladies' annual meeting at the clubhouse, attended by Mesdames Reece, Murray, Mayne, Patterson, Smedley and Gardner. Phyllis Mayne recorded the decision that as it was not possible to play any competitions or matches there was no point in electing a captain or secretary. Mrs Reece and Mrs Gardner were elected to represent the ladies on the main committee.

From that time until 1946 Mrs B.M. Adamson was captain, and slowly, as the scales of war tilted in favour of the allies, club life was restored. Gladys Reece the writer's mother, took over from Mrs Adamson and suddenly there were competitions galore in a gallant attempt to get back to normal.

Many obstructions had to be cleared. Much of the course was 'ornamented' with twelve foot concrete pillars, trees were cut down and placed across the fifth, sixth, 14th and 15th fairways and many pits were dug, all to the greater discouragement of German airmen. A barrage balloon unit and anti-aircraft guns were stationed on the second fairway.

Mrs Reece and her husband, Val, who was also a club member, had returned to Bristol in 1939 after twenty years in Durham county where their younger son, John, grew up. Val Reece was a well-known north country editor after some twenty years on Bristol papers from 1899.

Mrs Reece was an accomplished pianist, but took up golf on medical advice at the age of 40. She subsequently played for Durham county and was lady captain of Dinsdale Spa in the early 1930s.

John came home on leave in 1945, and in the mixed lounge of the old ramshackle clubhouse, and on the wrong side of the hatch, his mother introduced him to "a girl who can really play golf," – Peggy Millington. They married three years – and another tour abroad – later, and have been Henbury members ever since.

---

*Footnote*: Visit of Archie Compston for exhibition match. After lunch he addressed his putt on the tenth – and hit the ball backwards. Quiet consternation in the audience – Alan Fancote (reminiscences 1945).

*Above*, Club captain H.V.D. Trott presenting the Gloucestershire County championship trophy to Peggy Reece in 1952. Mrs Gwen Gotts, a leading Henbury ladies' member (right) was runner up. Looking on are Bertie Young, chairman, and Mrs Jane Bennett, the county ladies' president. *Right*, L.C. (Nick) Carter, first team captain, receiving the Western Daily Press League championship cup from John Reece, who was one of his team but represented the newspaper. Others, from left, are Tom Jones, George Dewfall, Bruce Gordon, Arthur Staniland, Arthur Skyrme and Jack Dutton (1956).

# Peggy Reece

In the next five decades one person more than any other kept the club's name in the public knowledge. This was evident even in recent weeks when Henbury cropped up in conversation and an international personality said: "Henbury? Ah, yes, Peggy Reece."

And at the end of a distinguished record in club, county and national golf, Peggy still goes out in great glee to play in a Grannies' match against the Rest and enjoys every minute of it playing off a handicap of three.

She first played for Gloucestershire in 1949 and retired from county play in 1990. She won ten county championships, the first in 1952 and the last in 1979, since when she lost in the 1982 final to Kitrina Douglas and in the 1987 final to Henbury's Ros Page at the 19th hole at Ross-on-Wye.

She captured five South Western Counties titles – 1952-59-63-68-71, and was a finalist eight times. She was runner-up to Ruth Porter in the all-Bristol final of the English championship in 1961, and was elected captain of England for the Home Internationals of 1966. With the latter honour went life membership of the club.

Peggy was an England selector in 1977 and chairman of selectors in 1980. She then became the first chairman of the Avon Schools Golf Association, and had much to do with the development of many youngsters of those days, Kitrina Douglas, Caroline Griffiths, the Shapcott sisters, and Avon boys as well.

She was twice captain of Gloucestershire, and Henbury ladies' captain in 1988. A series of course records stands to her credit. A 67 at Lansdown early in her career was followed by many others and a 69, 68 and ultimately 67 at Henbury, the latter in 1972. For many years she was plus one or two, and scratch most of the rest of the time.

Many good players and distinguished characters have graced the ladies' section down the years. Through the 1930s the best known were Mabel Pruett, whose husband Harry was popular in all Bristol golfing circles (The Pruett Salvers);

Mrs George Dudley, who never hit a shot beyond her limitations and was consequently very hard to beat; Zacyntha Frapwell, wife of F.J.R. never known by any name but Frappy; Gladys Willows, former captain, Daisy Gardner, Lilian Snook, Mrs Maggs, Mrs Tripp and F.J. Todd. Just before the non-playing idiot Hitler put an end to decent activities for a time, Mrs Dudley teamed up with Long Ashton professional Fred Jewell to win the Gloucester and Somerset Alliance foursomes from a record field of 132 with 67½ nett at Henbury.

The first post-war Alliance foursomes were at Henbury again, and Mrs Snook and D.A. Parsons won with 65 by one shot from Phyllis Mayne and her son John. Phyllis became ladies' captain, and her husband Cyril was club treasurer. She is still fit and well and living at Ferndown. Brenda Popplestone, three times Somerset champion from Knowle, joined Henbury and played for Gloucestershire from 1951. That year she helped her new club to a 'field day' in the Lady Marling at Henbury. Joyce Cumming, a club member with her husband Jock, a low handicap Scot who was a practising dentist, won the Marling Cup by four strokes with a nett 67. Brenda won the Scratch Cup with 86, two ahead of Gwen Gotts, another Henbury county player, and the home club also won both team championships.

Alan and Bess Fancote were well-known, having joined the club in 1945. Bess was twice captain, in 1953 and '55, when Mrs Stanley Hardiman was secretary. Bess, who was a keen tennis player, knew a thing or two about golf for she was a sister of England international Harley Roberts. The Fancotes now live in Seaton, Devon, but keep in touch. Other significant names at that time were Mrs Rose Major, Mrs Tim Campbell, captain in 1951–2, Mrs Norah Holley, whose husband Laurie and sons Roger and Michael were a good golfing trio, Mrs G. Murrell, Mrs Frank Noad and Joyce Warriner.

Back in 1932 Ruth Watson-Williams beat Mrs Windsor Aubrey in an all-Henbury final of the Gloucestershire championship at Failand. Ruth married Stanley Dickinson who was a leading Somerset player, but she retained her Henbury ties for many years before going finally to live at Burnham, winning the county title twice more, in 1947 and '51. Ruth and Peggy Reece won the Bristol and District Lady Golfer's Alliance Scratch Foursomes cup at Sham Castle in 1957, beating Christine Wills and Grace Bradley of Filton 2 and 1 over 36 holes, and again on other occasions.

On June 4th, 1957, Ruth Porter went round Henbury in 69 in the open meeting to equal Mrs Reece's record. They made a habit of it, those two . . .

*Far left*, Phyllis Lobbett, England international 1922–29. *Left*, Peggy Reece, England captain, 1966.

89

# Torch Bearers

Vivian Wilde has enhanced the ladies' section with a mixture of administrative expertise, official competence and social energy. She was Gloucestershire president in 1984, and is currently South Western Counties secretary. She was Henbury ladies' captain in 1975.

Rosalind Page was Dorset champion in 1981 before coming to live in Bristol and joining Henbury. Mrs Page was runner-up in the county championship in 1986, and won it the following year at Ross-on-Wye, beating Mrs Reece at the 19th.

Her husband Mike is an enthusiastic player, and a great calculating planner of the game. The Pages make a formidable foursome partnership.

Pat Skelton has been a county player for some years, and was county captain in 1988. She has many notable foursomes achievements to her credit, many in company with Mrs Reece in county matches, and she was runner-up in the county championship at Henbury last year.

The Henbury torch is carried now by Susan Elliott, daughter of David and Maura, the club's resident steward and stewardess whose record for service and catering is second to none.

In 1983 Susan was playing off 14 in Avon Schools events, but in the years since then she has won two county titles and come down to plus two before turning professional last autumn.

Susan won the South West Girls' championship at Kingsdown in 1985, and took her first title in 1988. She won again at Cirencester the following year when she was 21. After her first title she won the Marling after a tie with Mrs Reece.

She supported herself by taking a job in the hotel business, and tried hard to break through into the national amateur ranks. She tied with Lisa Walton for the Cotswold Gold Vase with a performance that brought her down to scratch in

1989, and last July she won the Bristol Ladies' Open championship by two shots with 144 at Mendip against a truly international field. In that same week she came fifth in a tournament at Stoke Poges, and then won the Bridget Jackson Bowl at Handsworth against Curtis Cup opposition from Vicki Thomas and Julie Hall.

These achievements did not lead to any national recognition, and Susan decided to join the W.P.G.A. which was what she had always had in mind. The club follows her activities with lively interest.

For the last four years Henbury ladies have won the county Scratch Foursomes title, and there are many truly competitive players, Mrs Jill McGregor, Mrs Sandra Waite, Mrs Marie Pilling, Mrs Louise Holwill and many more.

Sandra Waite has been heroine of many club quiz teams in inter-club competitions, and has revealed herself as a rules expert with a prodigious memory. Sandra and her husband John contribute much to the golfing and social life of the club, and both have been captains.

Vivian Wilde.

---

*Footnote*: The secretary was instructed to write a letter to Bristol Savages thanking them for their kindness in presenting a picture to the club (January 18, 1913).

*Far left*, Susan Elliot. *Left*, Craig Robinson. *Above*, Malcolm Lewis.

92

# A Silver Talent

At the age of 15 Malcolm Lewis, a Clifton College boy, was shooting scores like 66 at Henbury, 70 at Cotswold Hills, 71 at Minchinhampton and another record of 68 for Henbury's altered course. Alterations were thick and fast in those days. The year was 1974.

Two years later Malcolm sandwiched himself between Nick Faldo and Sandy Lyle in winning the British Youths' title with 277 at Gullane, a performance that included successive rounds of 65.

Malcolm is the son of the late Judge Sir Ian and Lady Marjorie Lewis, and it was clear that here was a special talent.

The City and County of Bristol championship was inaugurated at Henbury in 1960 when Malcolm was a year old, and when he won it in 1976 he was the first club member to do so. He had already captained England Boys, won the county junior title, the Ashton Vase and played for the senior county side.

After Clifton, he went to Bath University and, of course, led the golf team. He won the British Universities Stroke Play three times (1978-79-80) and the Match Play twice (1980-81). For three successive years he played for England in the Home Internationals, and against France in 1982. He won championships in Greece, India and Holland.

It followed naturally that he should play for Great Britain in the Walker Cup against America, but the glorious peak of an illustrious career was reached in the 1982 Open at Royal Troon when he won the Silver Medal as leading amateur and actually partnered the ultimate winner, Tom Watson, through the last two rounds.

A proud Henbury made him a life member.

By this time Peter Smith had established himself by winning the Ashmead Cup by seven strokes with a 68 gross, and he was only 15. Peter played some good golf throughout the 1970s, winning the county colts' title with two rounds of 74 at Lilley Brook in 1974, and many club events. Derek Hanson had won the Gloucestershire and the South Western

Counties colts' titles in one swoop at Knowle in 1967 at the age of 19.

In 1978 Peter Smith shattered the course record with 64 to win the Ashmead Cup again, and another of his best achievements was a record 68 in the second round to take the Burnham Challenge Cup with 142 in 1982.

The next talent to come to the fore was Craig Robinson, whose father, David, was club captain in 1983. On the eve of his 17th birthday in 1984, Craig won the county championship with 72 and 70 at Cirencester. He went to an American university on a golf scholarship but came back shortly afterwards and subsequently went to Stirling.

On the Ashmead Cup is the name of Aubrey Simons, former national table tennis champion and English international, who won it with 80-18-62 in 1986. Rhys Reed went round in 65-2-63 to finish second!

Reed and Ian Jones, winner of the historic Wimborne Cup in Dorset, in recent times, are probably the best of the current young players.

When the new clubhouse opened in 1959 it was considered fitting that the captain should drive himself into office, and Arthur Staniland was the first to do so.

Staniland was a remarkably effective player considering that his golfing education was picked up during his incarceration as an RAF officer in a German prisoner of war camp. Subsequently he paid a major role in club affairs and was chairman in the late 1970s. Arthur and his wife Millicent now live in Lincolnshire.

With a clubhouse second to none in the west country, the members turned their attentions to the course. The cry went up: How can we get rid of the long slog from the ninth tee to the top of the tenth? Everything had been tried before, but one more effort was made. The first four holes were played as they are now, followed by the seventh, eighth, ninth, sixth, fifth and tenth. It simply does not work.

The pop-up watering system costing £5,300 began to operate in 1972. The club profit that year was £2,700.

Two people who had done much for the club, Arthur Purnell and Lilian Snook, died that year.

On a happier note Suzanne Gibson returned from honeymooning with Stuart in time to partner Peggy Reece in the Kemp Omega open foursomes at Long Ashton. They were the only feminine partnership in a field of 170, and they won with 67 nett, Sue holing a chip for a birdie four at the last. There was an additional bonus for Henbury in the victory of John and Sandra Waite in the mixed tournament.

*Left*, Douglas Marshman. *Centre*, Bill Naish. *Right*, Bill Scapens.

In 1975 Henbury staged the British Girls' Open Amateur championship, and Sue Cadden beat Lisa Isherwood 4 and 3 in the final. Chairman Herbert Brook made much of them, and they all loved him.

In 1977 a development project was approved for a new lounge and changing room for the ladies, and alterations to the living quarters of the steward and stewardess, David and Maura Elliott, who joined the staff in 1974. It is Henbury's extreme good fortune that they are still here.

The work was done within the year, and in his chairman's report of 1978 Staniland said "Much good has been achieved and the work done within the estimate". The next morning Vic Hill drove himself in as captain, escorted to the first tee by a detachment of Royal Marines who were delighted to get their hands on him again. Hill succeeded George Houlden whose Jubilee Year success in office ended with a club presentation to mark his own wedding aniversary.

Houlden was an all-rounder who played rugby for BAC and was capped for Bristol just after the war. He was also captain of BAC cricket. He played golf as a boy on Clifton Down, and joined Henbury in 1946. It was George who gave the club the hickory mashie niblick made by Jack Branch, which is now used as a medal trophy. It is a memorial to a popular man who died in 1988.

In the chair in recent years Basil Gale, Stuart Gibson and W.E. 'Nobby' Clark proved no-nonsense men of wide experience. Gale, a former police chief, takes the club into its second century as its president. He has the outstanding record of having held every office the club's administration entails.

Gibson joined in 1952. He had played cricket and golf in his native Devon, and more golf in Lancashire during a career in Customs and Excise. He held most Henbury offices, and was captain in 1971, and later captain of Captains in the Gloucestershire Society. He had a strong code of ethics and sportsmanship, backed by a sparkling humour. Nobby Clark is one of the same ilk.

The club has been blessed with Scots influence on odd occasions in its history but never more so than in the captaincy of Lewis Stuart Black in 1972.

He arrived here in 1961 with an impressive pedigree of golf – having started to play in 1923 as a junior at the now defunct Busby and Clarkston course until 1926. He then joined Largs and stayed until 1946 concurrently with membership at East Renfrewshire from 1932 until coming here. In 1932 he was down to scratch.

Until a year ago, equipped with two new hips, Lewis was 16, but he has had a cycle of health problems in the last season, particularly regarding his hands, and to crown it all he fell heavily on the clubhouse steps last October and broke a shoulder.

His career as a golfer ended with the presidency of the Gloucestershire County Union in 1987.

\* \* \*

In his ninetieth year Winchcombe made history at Henbury by hitting a ball so far it couldn't be seen. 'I think it fell on the green,' he announced but had to end up looking in the bushes behind. When he couldn't find it, he went off in disgust to drive from the next tee. Winchcombe hates to lose a ball and was further irritated when the players coming up behind shouted to attract his attention.

'What's the matter?' he muttered impatiently to his companion who was walking the course with him.

The men came across. 'Have you lost a ball?' they asked. 'Yes' answered Winchcombe shortly.

'It's in the hole!' they replied . . .

Winchcombe Howard Hartley Lansdowne was a great Bristolian Quaker who had a career with the Bristol Waterworks and spent the rest of his life doing good things for and on behalf of people.

He joined Henbury in 1935, and in her delightful book Winchcombe Remembers, Mary I Williams portrays a wonderful philanthropist with a bubbling sense of humour.

Winchcombe played golf on his ninety-ninth birthday but died in the following year.

\* \* \*

By a happy coincidence Henbury's Douglas Marshman is president of Gloucestershire during the club's centenary.

This is a peak in the sporting career of a man who has been a leader wherever he has gone in life. Not many come to be captain of more than one golf club, but Doug was captain of Painswick in 1960, and Henbury 15 years later.

He has been a member of Stinchcombe Hill, the old club at Ross-on-Wye and Long Ashton, with country membership since 1955 of Clyne, the famous old course near Swansea. His lowest handicap has been four and now, as he enters his seventies, he is off eleven.

Doug was educated at Bristol Grammar School, and destined for the 'rag trade'. This did not appeal, and he became a regular soldier in 1939 in Royal Artillery. He was commissioned in 1943 and a year later was seconded to Ministry of Supply.

He returned to regimental duty after the war as battery commander in Singapore, played rugby and hockey, and captained the Army and Combined Services swimming and water polo teams.

When his service career ended he went into insurance, reaching another peak in Bristol with Commercial Union.

\* \* \*

As recently as 1981 there was a minor revolution when members threw out a committee proposal for clubhouse improvements, and a small group with majority backing put counter measures forward which were adopted. *Bristol Illustrated* reported:

> Architect Cyril Hill's design suited the pocket, Bensons the builders moved in and Andrew Besant, a club member of seemingly endless electrical stimulus in all he does, took over management of light and power. In his capacity as an electrical engineer, club captain 'Nobby' Clark gave invaluable advice, and the work went ahead so fast that everything was done well ahead of the deadline.

It is not given to every man that he should come into office at the century stage, but John Leeming from Nottingham has done so in taking over from Jack Estill, and the members will wish their new secretary well.

Estill retired last November after some nine-and-a-half years, which he thought – and hoped – was a record, but he was outdone by the late Major Wilkins, of the 1930s, who held office for more than eleven years. Jack has described

*Left*, Stuart Gibson. *Centre*, Jack Estill. *Right*, Lewis Black.

himself as a 'workaholic' and members can vouch for it. He joined the club in 1970 and took over as secretary in 1981 on the retirement of Dick Hamilton, the quiet one with the ready smile, another sportsman who played soccer for the Admiralty at Bath, cricket for the South West Regional Health Authority, and enjoyed swimming, tennis and golf, not necessarily in that order.

Bill Naish was born in Bristol but boarded at the Royal Pinner School from the age of seven, then served in the Wiltshire Regiment based in Germany. On returning to civilian life, he joined the family wholesale tobacco business established by his grandfather in 1919. He married Janet in 1956 and has a married son and daughter. He has been a member of Henbury Golf Club, together with his wife, since 1978, and readily admits that he is still trying to obtain a respectable handicap. He is known amongst friends for his caricatures and confesses to a passing interest in wine.

Twenty-three years ago Bob and Beatrice Harvie came down from Glasgow, and before they really knew what was happening they were members of Henbury. It was a good thing for the club. To listen to Bob's Scots and to realise that he played off five, is to understand that he knows a great deal about golf.

He played regularly for the first team in the Bristol League, and then became non-playing captain. He was club captain in 1980, taking over from Eric Innes, a north countryman who had a course record 68 to his credit and is now chairman of the greens committee. Bea Harvie was ladies' captain in 1982.

Bob Harvie is one of the most enthusiastic team supporters and club men it is possible to meet, and it is good fortune to have him as chairman for the centenary occasion.

---

*Footnote*: Bristol Clergy Golfing Society were one player short when they visited Henbury and 'borrowed' the Rev. Hookham. He beat F.H. Moss by one hole, but the clergy were beaten 5–3, one of their better results. They have been having a hard time! (1924).

# Things are Different

One day last October Miss Skyrme walked into a village shop and bumped into William Dent, a lifelong acquaintance, and told him of the author's quest for information about the early days of the club.

Earlier reference is made to Bill Dent in the story of the artisans' section. He is now in his eighty-fifth year, but he went home from the shops that day, sat down and composed this:

> Henbury, a real sporty course that has seen many alterations in its time. During the first World War two or three of its holes were ploughed up, and wheat, etc, grown. But to start off really about the club . . . It had a lovely clubhouse and putting green that set the place off.
>
> As to the playing part of it – there were some really tough holes namely the Windmill Hole and the notorious dog leg hole between the woods.
>
> The bottom of the course, the lower nine was altered more than once, and the old Windmill Hole green was close to the old Canford Lane. But that hole and the next were out after the land was developed. Bungalows and houses with lovely long gardens finished that.
>
> But now to more olden times . . . The fairways and grass was all cut by horse mower. I personally felt sorry for the horse and man. The 13th and 14th fairways must have been very tiring to both of them. That was a long time ago and things are much different now.
>
> To talk about the golfers now, and Henbury Club had some well-known names in the books. I can remember Sir George Riseley and many more that played the Top Nine, as it was called. Miss Phil Lobbett, the woman international, used to play at Henbury. But her home was only just across the road at the top of

the Hill. And the time came for the working chaps of Westbury to join the Artisan Association. I personally joined and it was a really wonderful experience to own a Bag of Clubs and to be able to play on the course on Mondays, Weds and Sunday mornings up to 11 o'clock. They were wonderful times.

Now back to older times again . . . The caddies fees were 9d a round and to find a few balls in the rough and woods was something very good especially if it was a new Silver King. But as the years progressed there were more alterations and holes were made different. The Cherry Orchard part improved things a lot and the course today is still very enjoyable.

The pro in the 1920s and 30s was Mr Jack Branch. His son Billy became a good pro. There was always a lot of theatre people who liked playing at Henbury. I can remember the singer Richard Blamey and his friends from the Princes Theatre who were playing the beautiful Lilac Time. They all agreed it is a pleasant and interesting course but as the years go on I suppose the cost of Balls, Clubs and Subs have changed very much. But that applies to all sports to-day.

But going back many years I still talk to other old timers who remember Henbury, and we always will. So hoping I have written as much as I can put together. I hope it is satisfactory for you. I am, yours faithfully

Mr Dent.


Thus, Mr Dent, who has lived through all but fifteen years of the Henbury history, can bring to a close the first story of Golf on the Hill.

*Footnote*: "We have not any play on our links today, so there are no results to publish; but just elaborate a little on the weather conditions." – Telephone message from the club to 'Bunker' of the *Evening News* (December 8th, 1913).

# Epilogue

The final pages of *Golf On The Hill* were completed at noon on October 30th, 1990. The manuscript was to go to the publisher the following day, and the author was happy the deadline had been met. No epilogue was necessary.

The essential records of the club had been lost in the 1959 fire that consumed the old clubhouse. Nothing was on record between 1898 and 1960 apart from ladies' logbooks and the minutes of Henbury Properties. The former yielded little beyond immaculately preserved competition results, and some minutes, and the latter were purely financial, dry as dust, repetitive statements. Effectively, there was no access to sources.

Research of such a subject in the basement of Bristol Reference Library cannot be the ordered and precise making of notes from a handily placed, leather bound, well-loved volume of historical fact. Rather is it the task of a coal heaver in the oldest working clothes in a musty atmosphere, bent double over dusty, and in many cases tattered, volumes of monstrous size, the reading of which demands the physical contortions of the same heaver at a coal face long ago.

Inquiries into Henbury's past carried the researcher the length and breadth of the country, adding greatly to the coffers of British Telecom and the Post Office.

Nevertheless, the work was done, and the author was reasonably satisfied that within the limits of space there had not been too much omission.

He picked up the telephone . . .

\* \* \*

That morning Jack Estill, friendliest of men, was busy preparing the way for his successor, John Leeming, and among other things decided to 'spring clean' the stationery cupboard at the top of the steps to the office.

Behind the shelves stacked with paper, envelopes, paper clips, elastic bands and all the paraphernalia that goes with administration, there was a dim, cave-like recess he had never entered. He remembered there was a box of sorts in there, "full of old invoices," he had been told.

"Let's have it out," he exclaimed, scattering the dust of decades and disturbing a long line of well bred spiders.

He prised the box open, started with shock and rose slowly to his feet. He gazed down at the contents, aghast, unbelieving.

The telephone rang . . . John Reece wanted a quick word.

Jack picked up the instrument and said slowly:

"I don't know how to say this . . ." There was a pause. Then "I'VE JUST FOUND THE RECORDS!"

Silence. Unbelieving, stunned silence. He went on:

"All those records that were lost in the fire, they're here. In a box. They've been here all the time . . ."

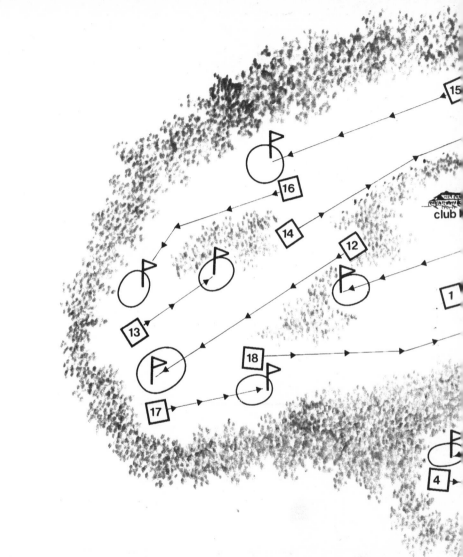

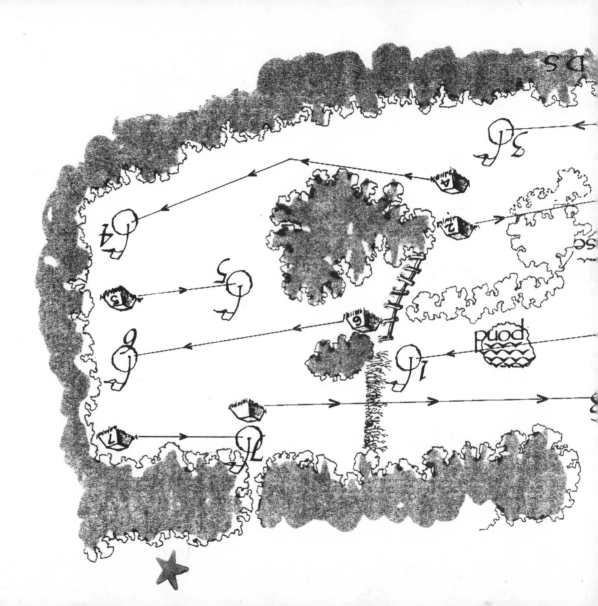